After Bruegel

by Samuel McNair

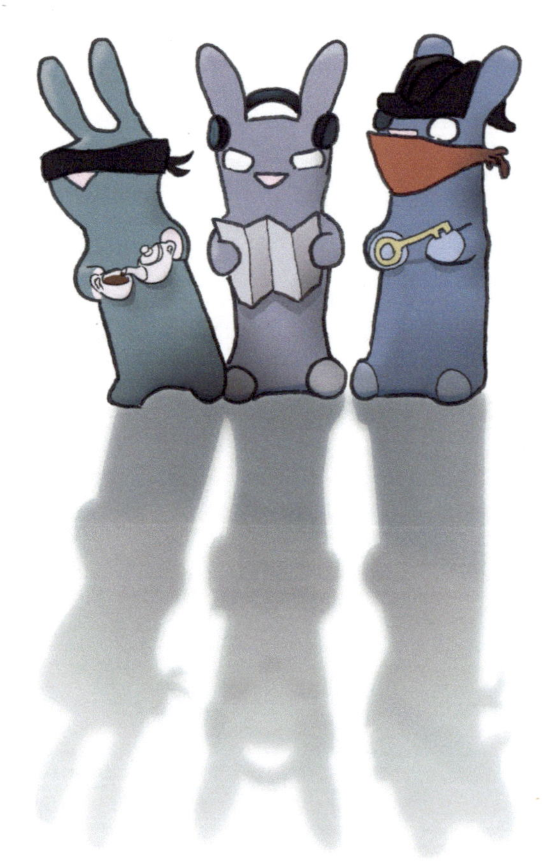

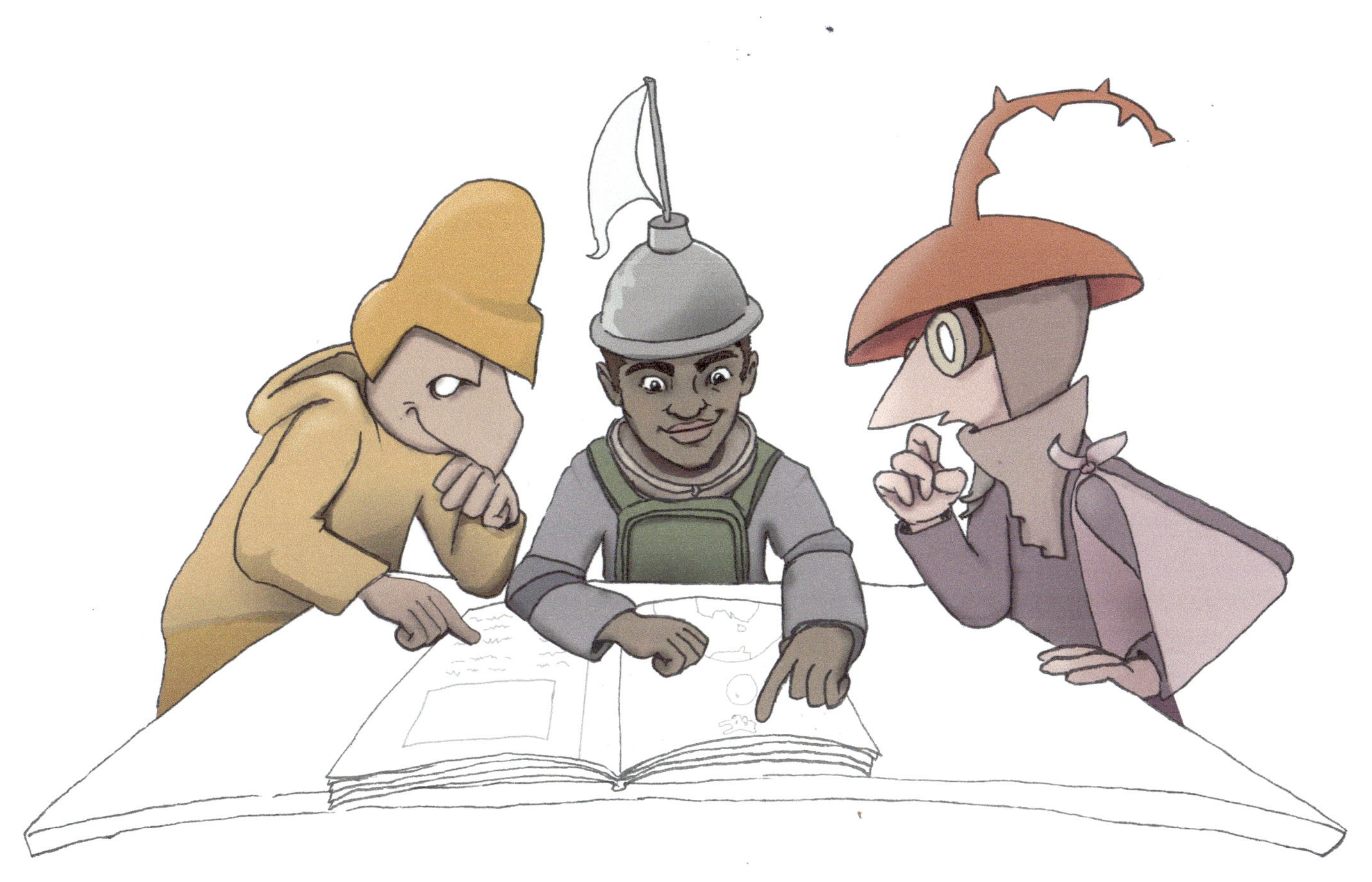

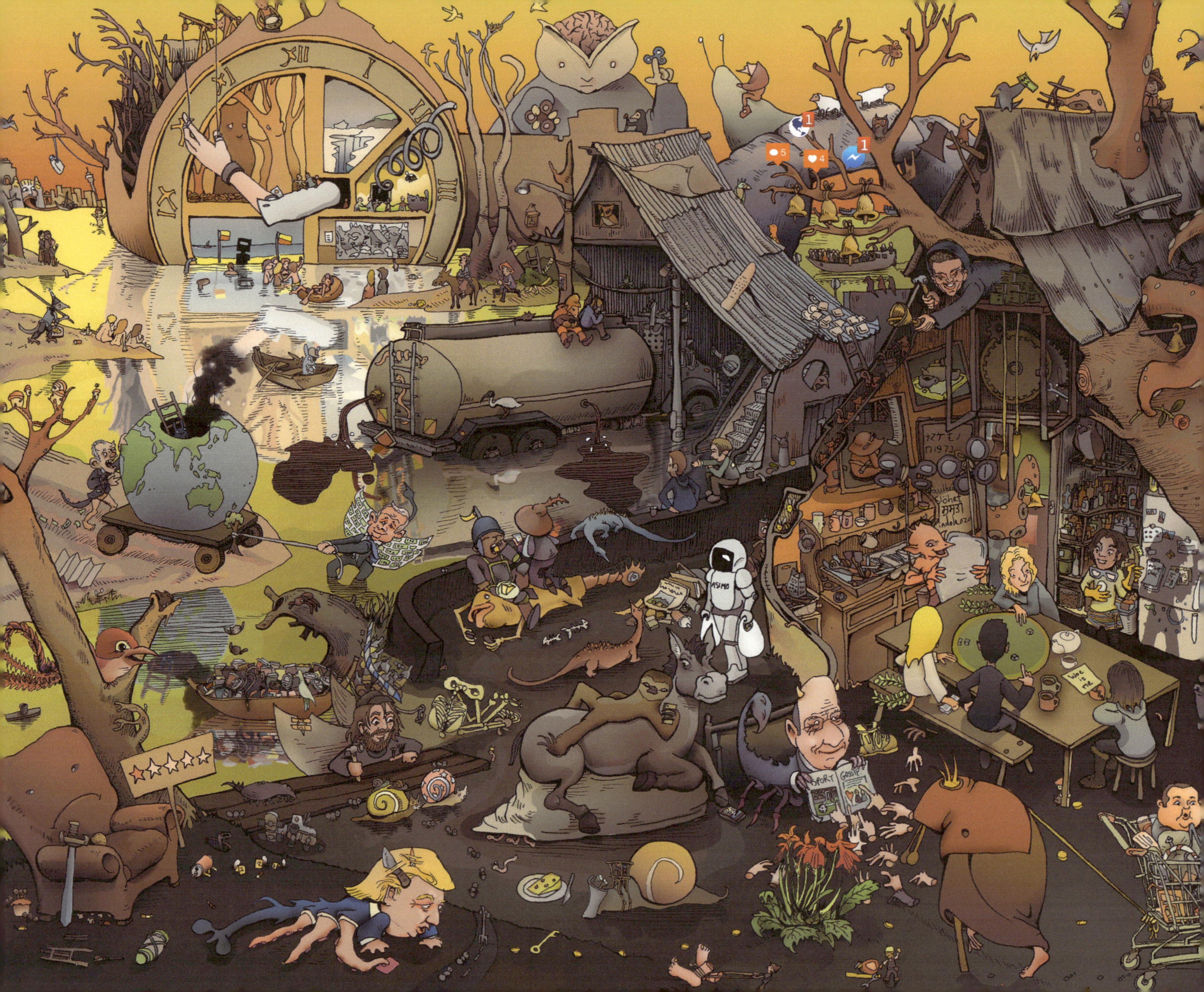

ASIMO
Slöhet
indolenza
Woe is me
SPORT
GOSSIP

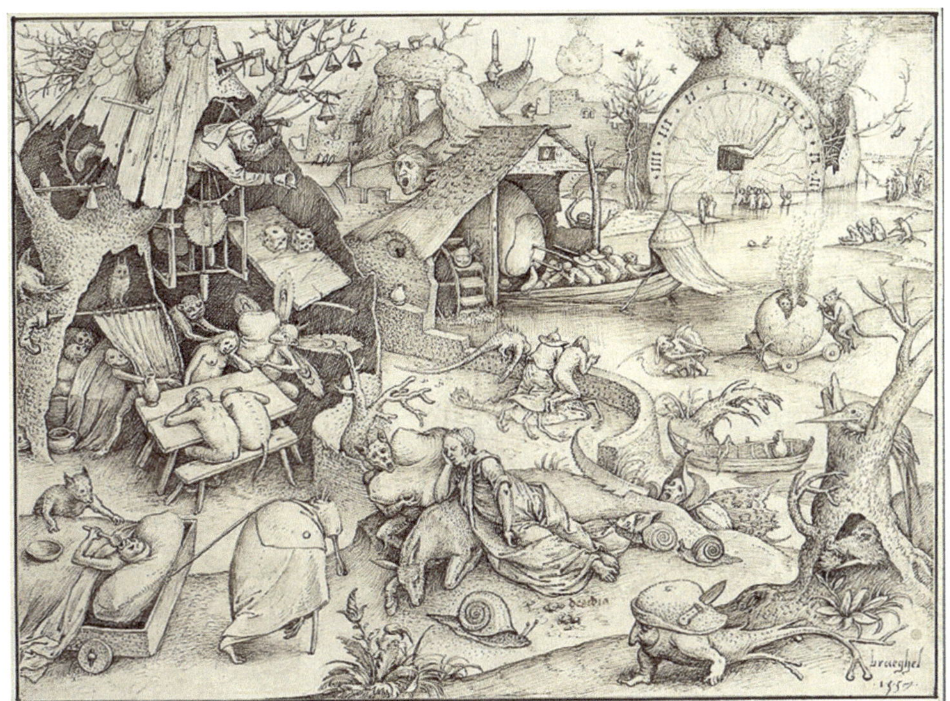

Pieter Bruegel the Elder, Sloth (Desidia), 1557

Lazy bones
Can't lift a finger
Dragging your feet
Resting on your laurels
Devil makes work for idle hands
Passing the buck
Armchair warrior
Bad workers blame their tools
Running out of time
Passing time
Hand of time
Counting eggs before they hatch

Armchair critic
Band-aid solution
Couch potato
Spannner in the works
Head in the sand
Hands are tied
The walls have ears
Fork in the road
Message in a bottle
Cheap skates
Could not get off his ass
Beer crimes

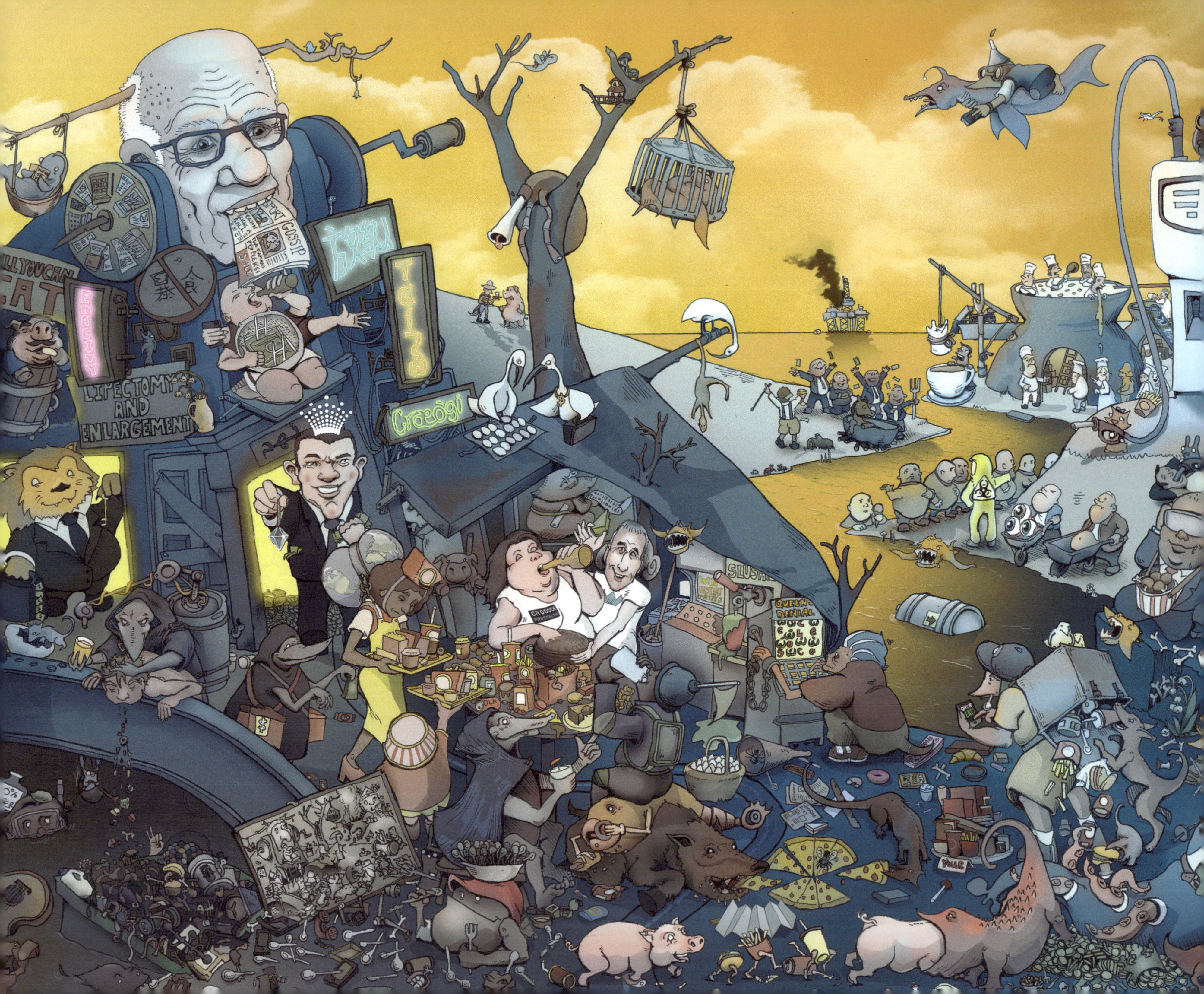

LIPECTOMY AND ENLARGEMENT
EDACITY
SPORT
PERSON KICKS A BALL
GOSSIP
TWO FAMOUS PEOPLE KISS
SALE
WIN INSTANT PRIZES
QUEEN DENIAL

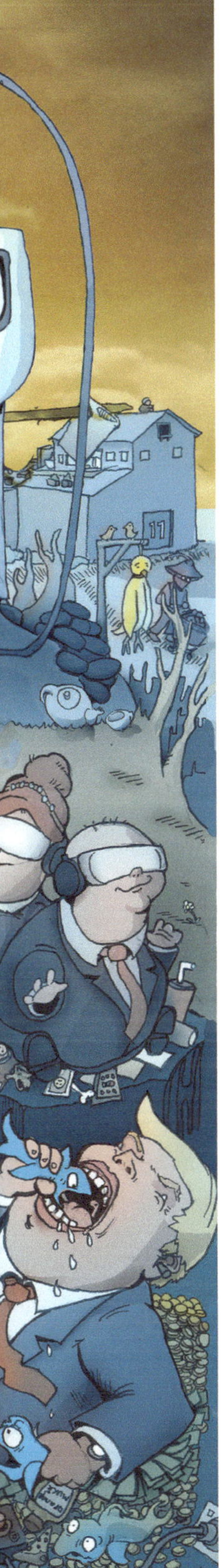

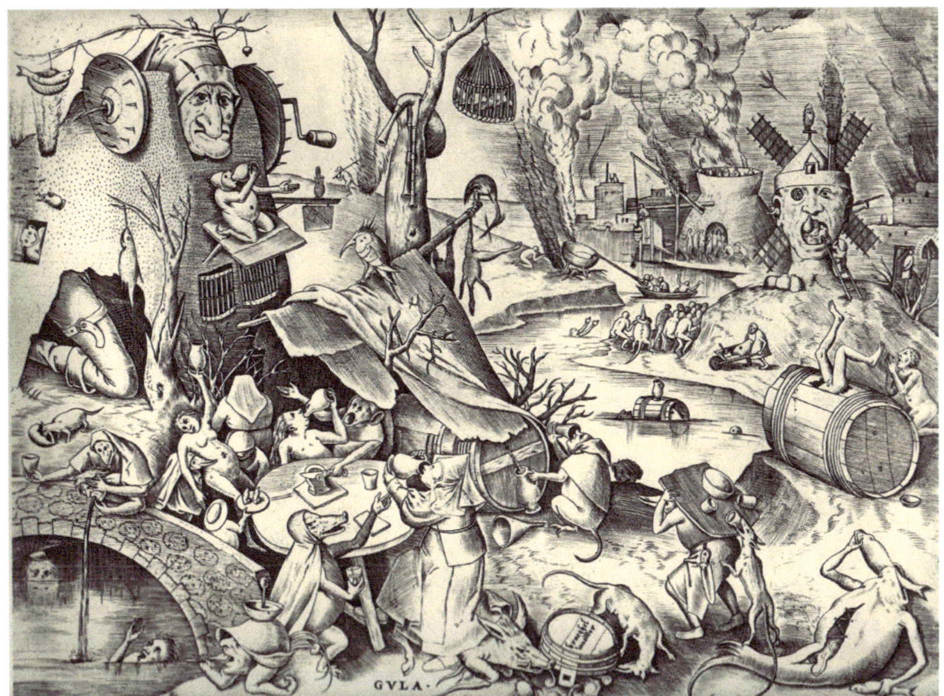

Pieter Bruegel the Elder, Gluttony (Gula), 1558

Icing on the cake
Fast food
His eyes are bigger than his stomach
Bitten off more than you can chew
So hungry they could eat a horse
Sweet tooth
Too many chefs ruin the broth
Ball park figure
All your eggs in one basket
Bottom of the barrel
World on your shoulders

A lot on your plate
Water under the bridge
Skeleton in your closet
Peer pressure
Road hog
Home sick
Drink like a fish
Fat cat
Cup runneth over
Speak of the devil

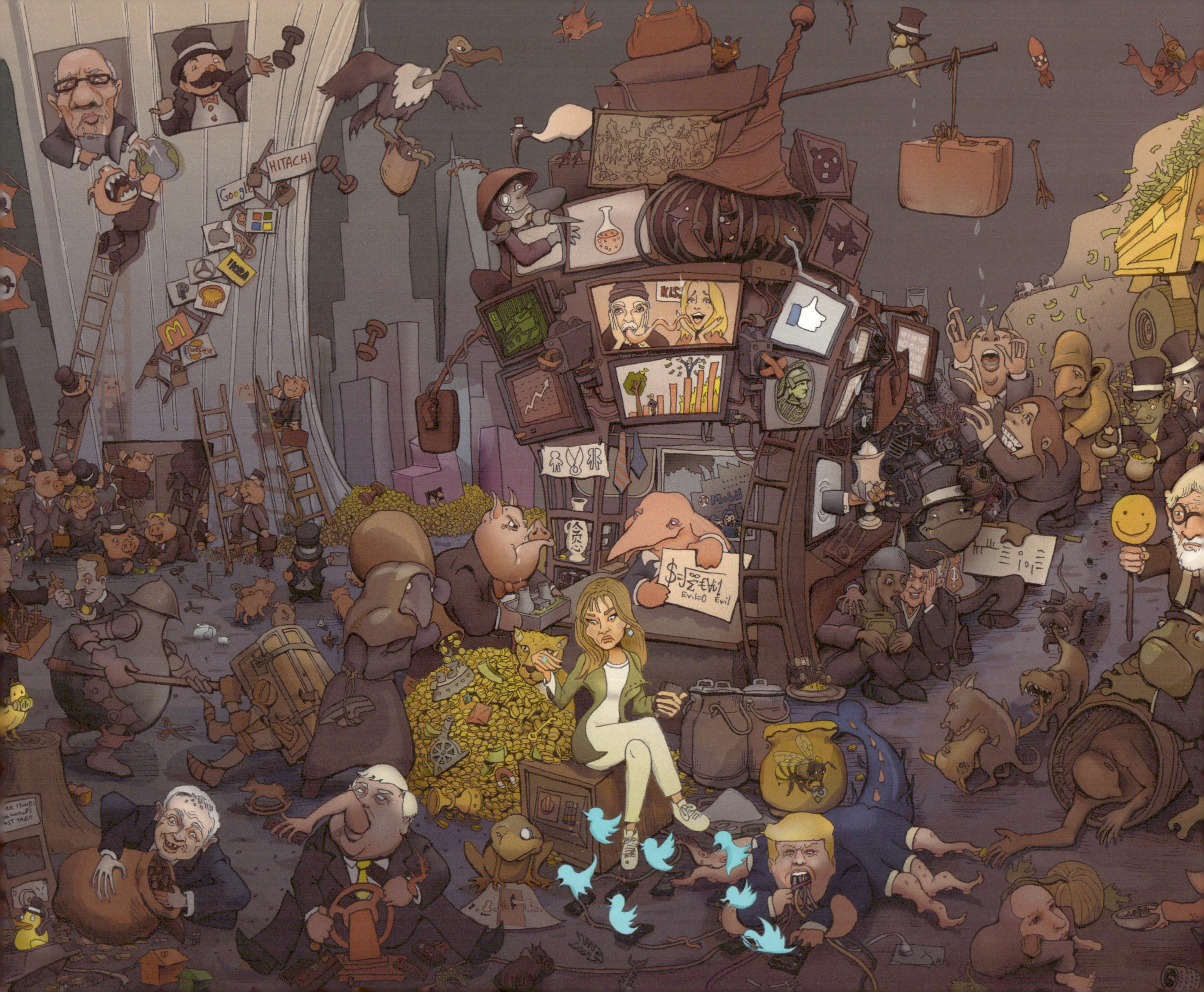
HITACHI
Google
IKEA
BURGER
Mobil
$=∫Σ∞ €∀i1
Evil=0 Evil

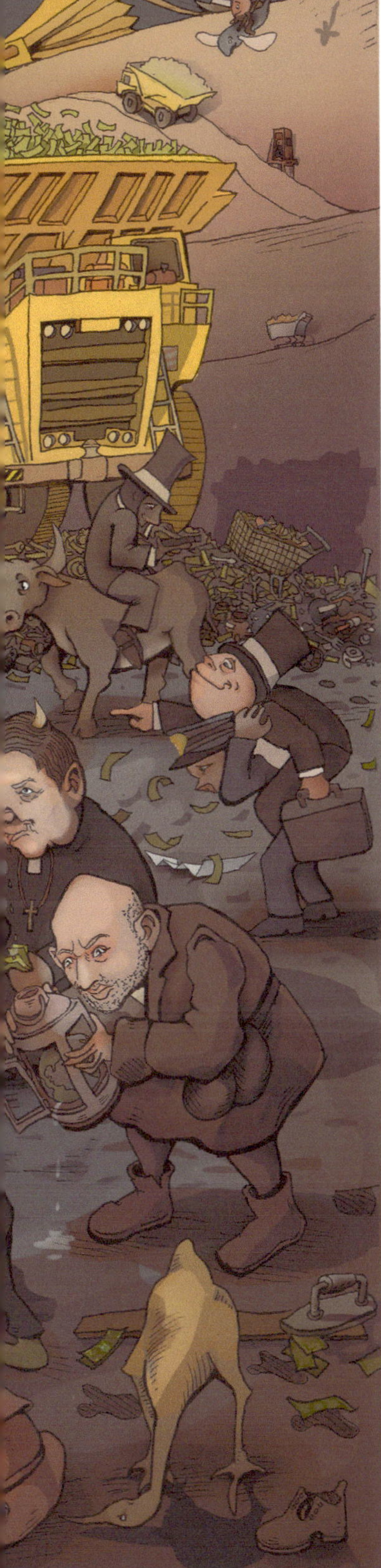

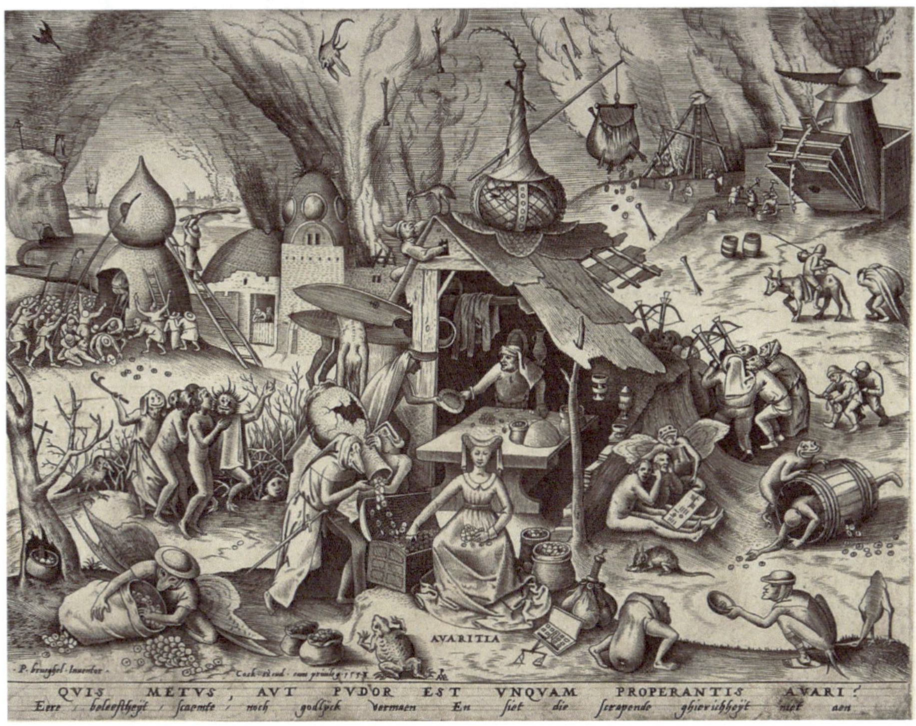

Pieter Van der Heyden after Pieter Bruegel the Elder, Avarice (Avaritia), 1558

Money is the root of evil
Corporate ladder
Control freak
Devil's advocate
Vulture never drops it's chicks
Dog eat dog eat dog
Pig headed
Trickle down
Piggie back

Power hungry
Pig-mail
Milk and honey
Ride the bull backwards
Thief of thieves
Throwing your weight around
A foot in the door
Something up your sleeve
Truckload of cash

Long fingers - Långa fingrar
The hand comes out of their throat - Nodo kara te ga deru

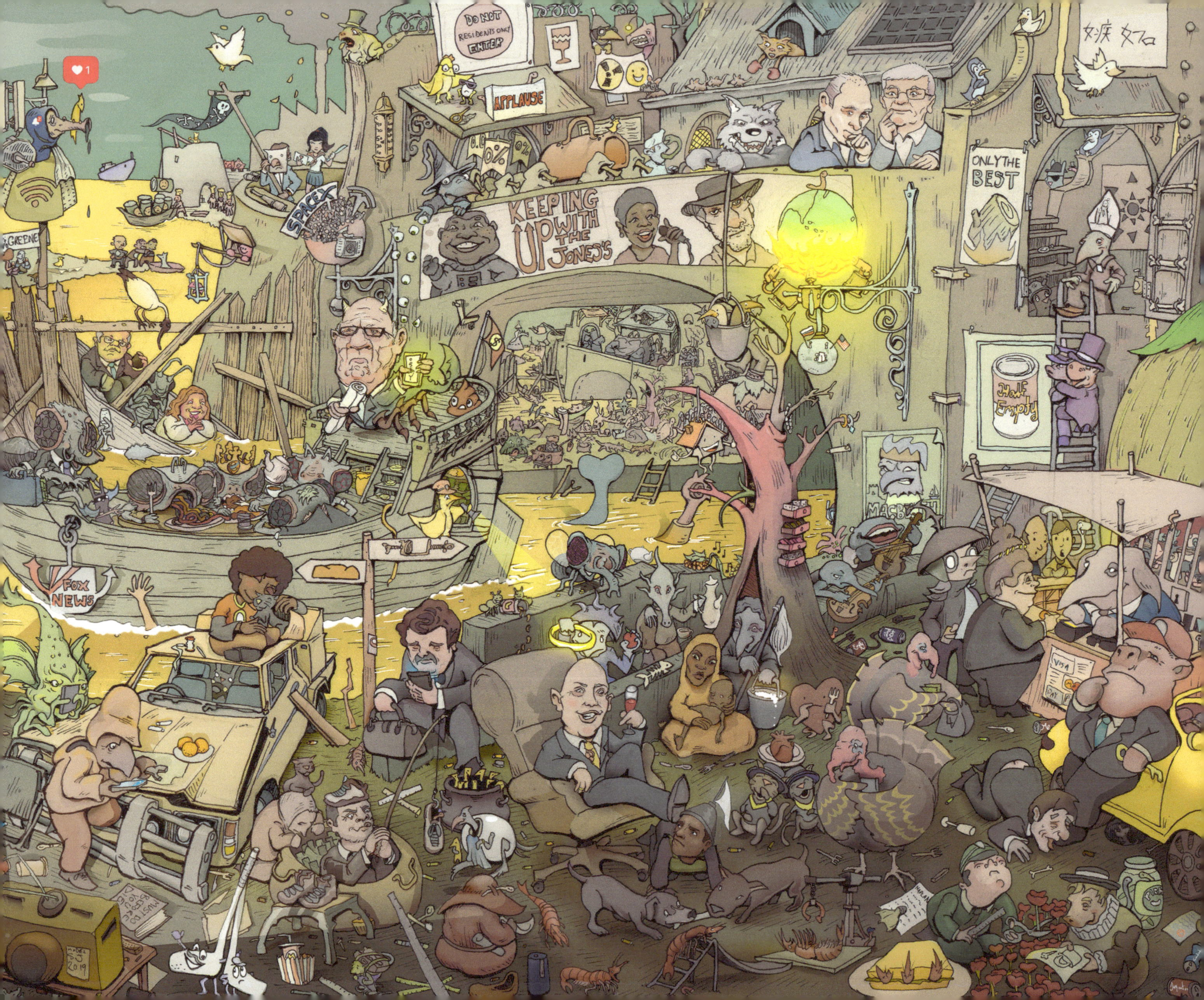
DO NOT ENTER
RESIDENTS ONLY
APPLAUSE
SPACEX
KEEPING UP WITH THE JONES'S
ONLY THE BEST
Half Empty
FOX NEWS
VISA

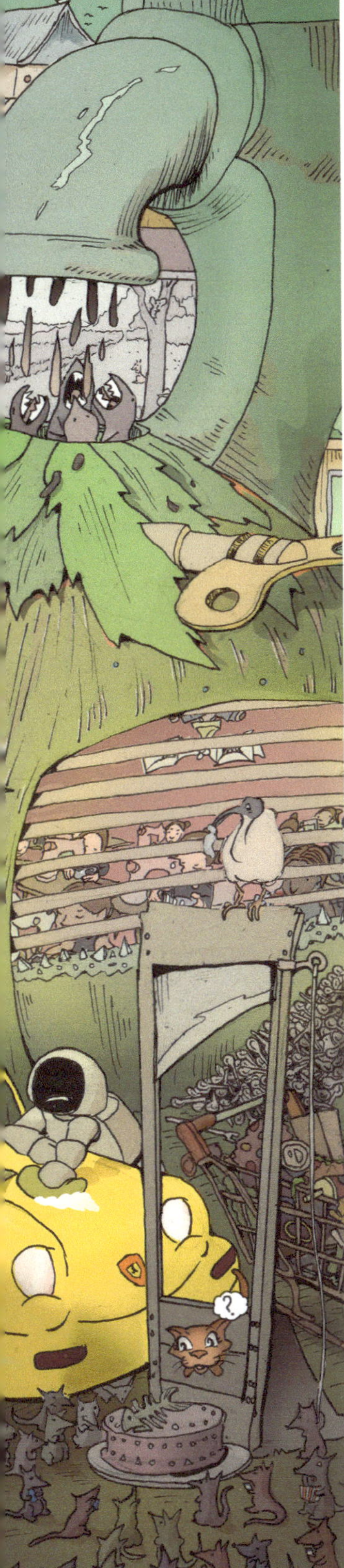

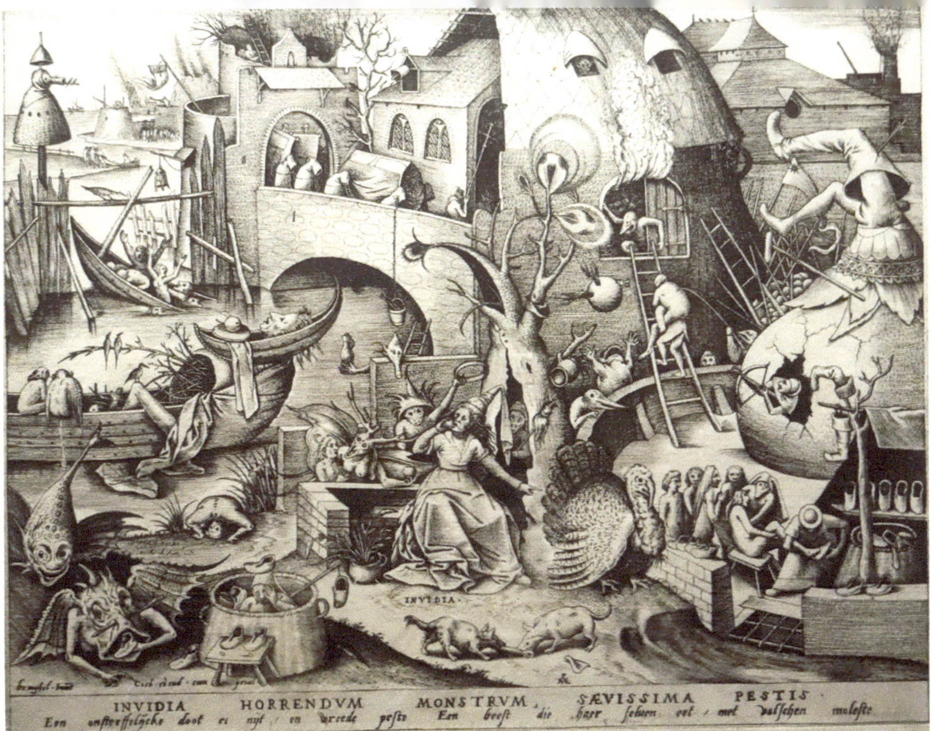

Pieter Van der Heyden after Pieter Bruegel the Elder, Envy (Invidia), 1558

A cat in mittens catches no mice
Apples and oranges
Chalk and cheese
Hockey dad
Foam at the mouth
Fly on the wall
Stick in the mud
Let the cat out of the bag
Curiousity killed the cat
Green eyed monster
Heard it through the grapevine
Play second fiddle
Spill the beans
Back-seat driver
Boot-licker
World-in-flames

Grass is always greener
Casting envious eyes
Sticky-beak
Poop deck
Happy home
Shine a light on
News anchor
The Jones'
Spit on a dove
Space race
Piggy-back
Eat your heart out
Tall poppy syndrome
Under lock and key
Needle and thread

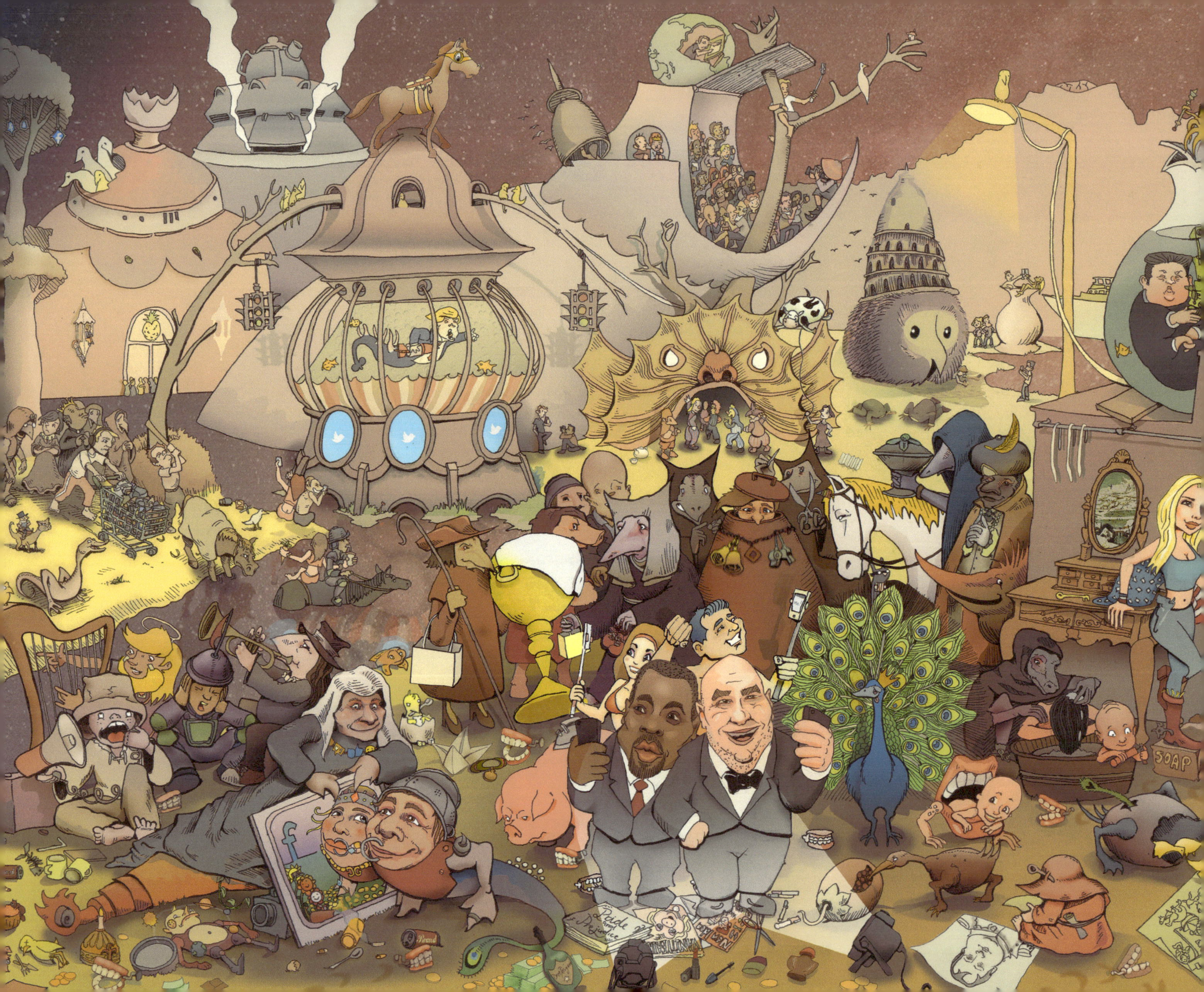

Pride and Prejudice
SOAP

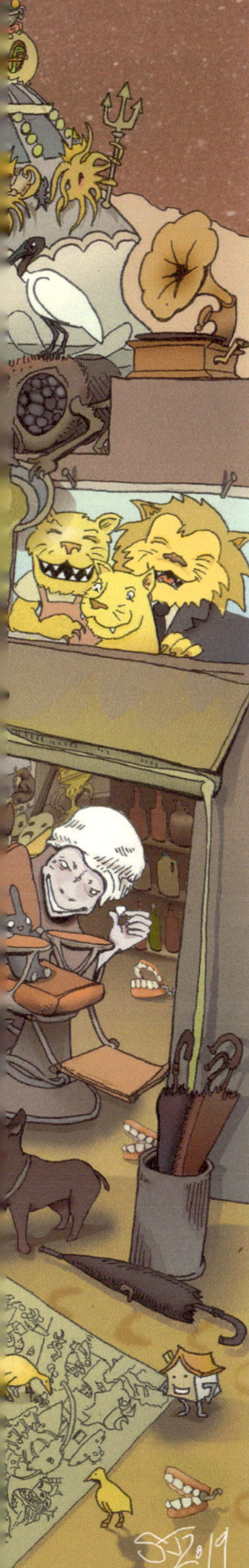

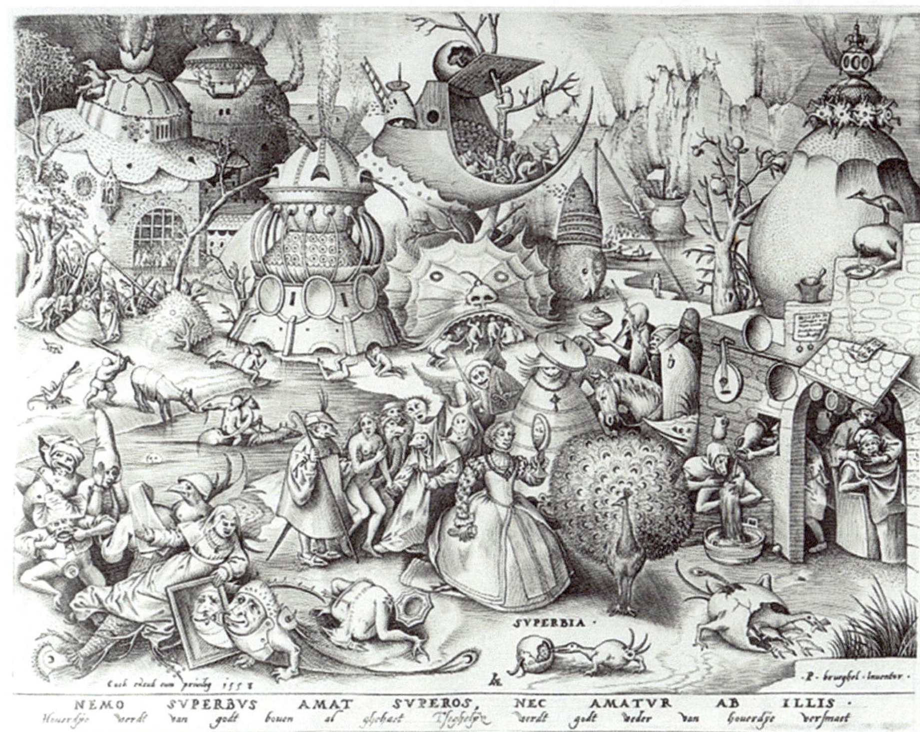

Pieter Van der Heyden after Pieter Bruegel the Elder, Pride (Superbia), 1558

High horse
A feather on one's head (على راسه ريشه)
Bells and whistles
Blow your own trumpet
Born with a silver spoon in one's mouth
Bury your head in the sand
Swollen head
Proud as a peacock (Etre fier comme un coq)
Universe revolves around you (umblecist)
Inflating a cow (吹牛)
Hay in your boots (foin dans ses bottes)
Born from a mouth (Kuchi kara umareta)
Harping on
House proud

A vanity (dressing table)
Pride of lions
Pride and prejudice
Chatterbox
Soap box
Fools rush in
Trophy spouse
The early worm
Carrot and the stick
Fish out of water
Steaming hot
Influencers
Pearls before swine

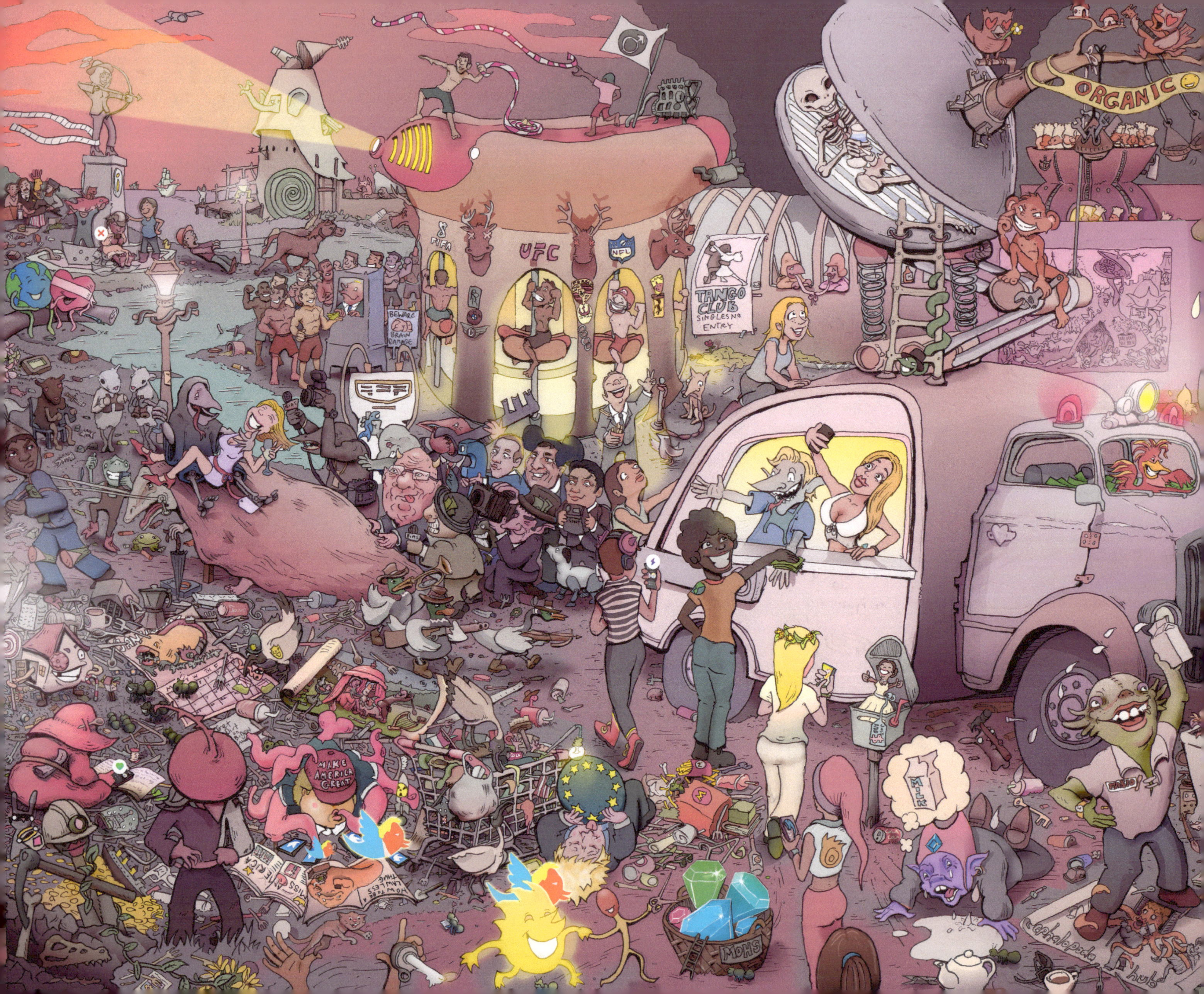
ORGANIC
FIFA
UFC
NFL
TANGO CLUB
SINGLES NO ENTRY
BEWARE BRAIN DAMAGE
MAKE AMERICA GREAT
HOW TO BE A LAWLESS THUG
MILK
MOHS
cephalopoda hub

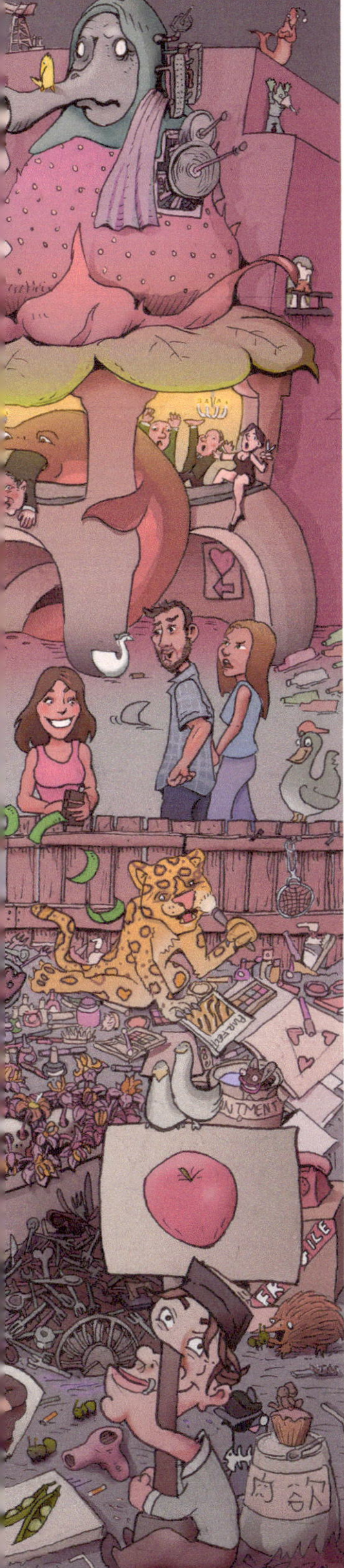

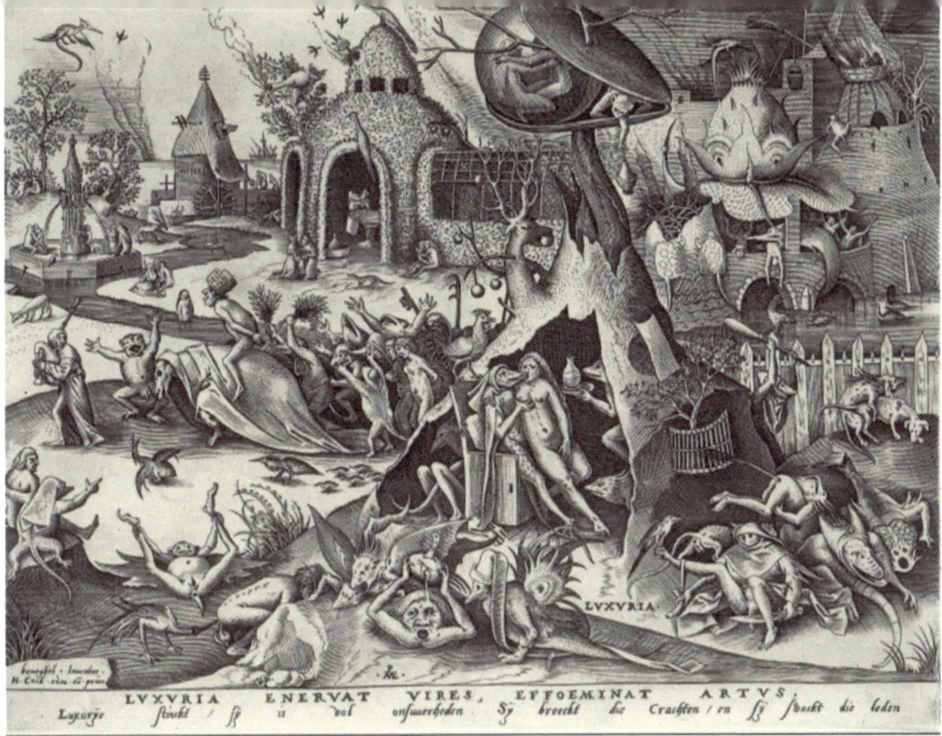

Pieter Van der Heyden after Pieter Bruegel the Elder, Lust (Luxuria), 1558

All the world loves a lover
Can't stop being the owl
When dogs were tied with sausages...
Love is blind / L'amour est aveugle
Don't let grass grow on your feet
Have a chip on one's shoulder
Like two peas in a pod
To wrap your head around something
Throw caution to the wind
The elephant in the room
To get out of hand
Hold your horses
Duck hunt
It takes two to tango
The ship has sailed
A leopard cannot change its spots

Home sweet home
Fools seldom differ
Getting tongue-tied
Mail order bride
Playing hard to get
Distracted boyfriend meme
Fly in the ointment
Tunnel of love
Too hard basket
Playing with fire
Gold digger
Black sheep
Tears over spilt milk
Fashion victim
Running with scissors
Looking sheepish

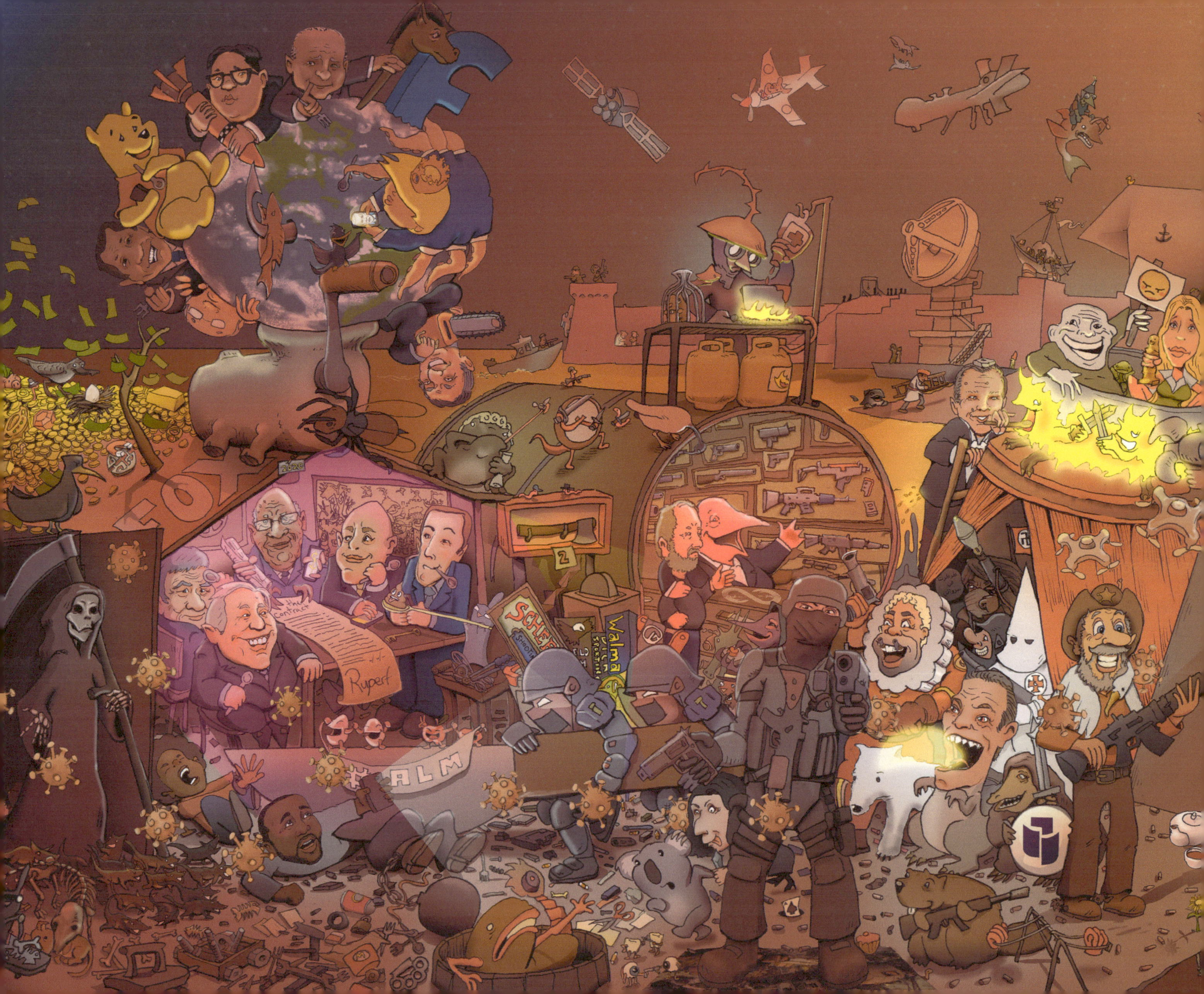
FOX
the Contract
Rupert
2
SCHER
Walma
ALM

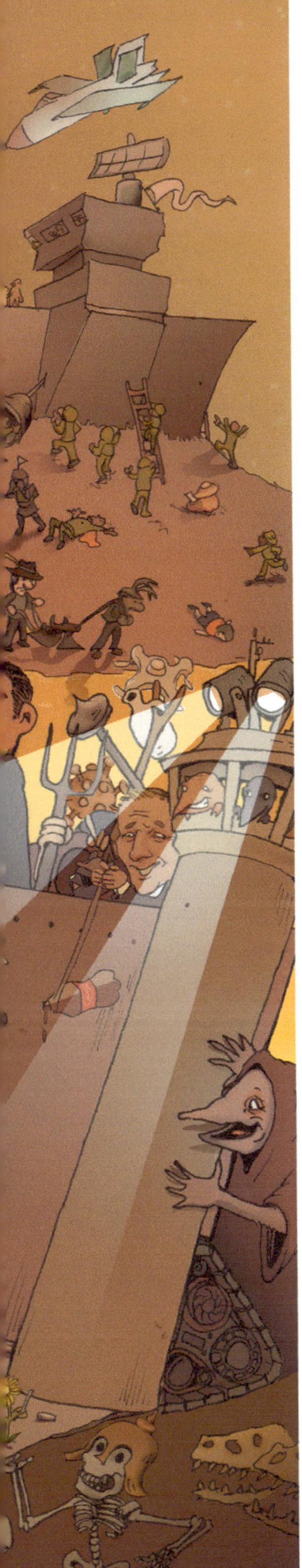

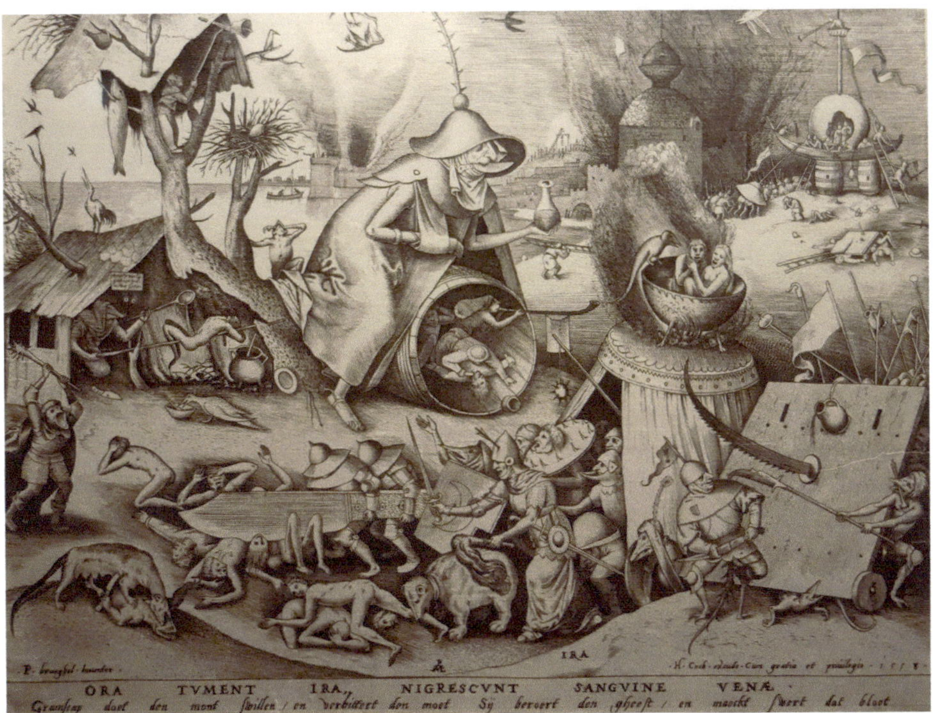

Pieter van der Heyden after Pieter Bruegel the Elder, Anger (Ira), 1558

Swinging fists
Fan the flames
Fight against time
Fight fire with fire
An axe to grind
Make blood boil
Feed the fire
An eye for an eye

A tooth for a tooth
Devil's contract
Cooking with gas
Piggy bank
Eager beaver
Ace in the hole
Like shooting fish in a barrel

Breath fire
Rage quit
Driving up the wall
Pushing up the daisies
Who sups with the Devil,
should have a long spoon
Death's door
Blood on their hands

To excrete embers अंगारे उगलना

Laws catch flies but let hornets go free Алтынного вора вешают, а полтинного чествуют

[For every] one with a plow — [there's] seven with a spoon Один с сошкой — семеро с ложкой.

Every sandpiper praises its own swamp Vsyak kulik svoyo boloto khvalit

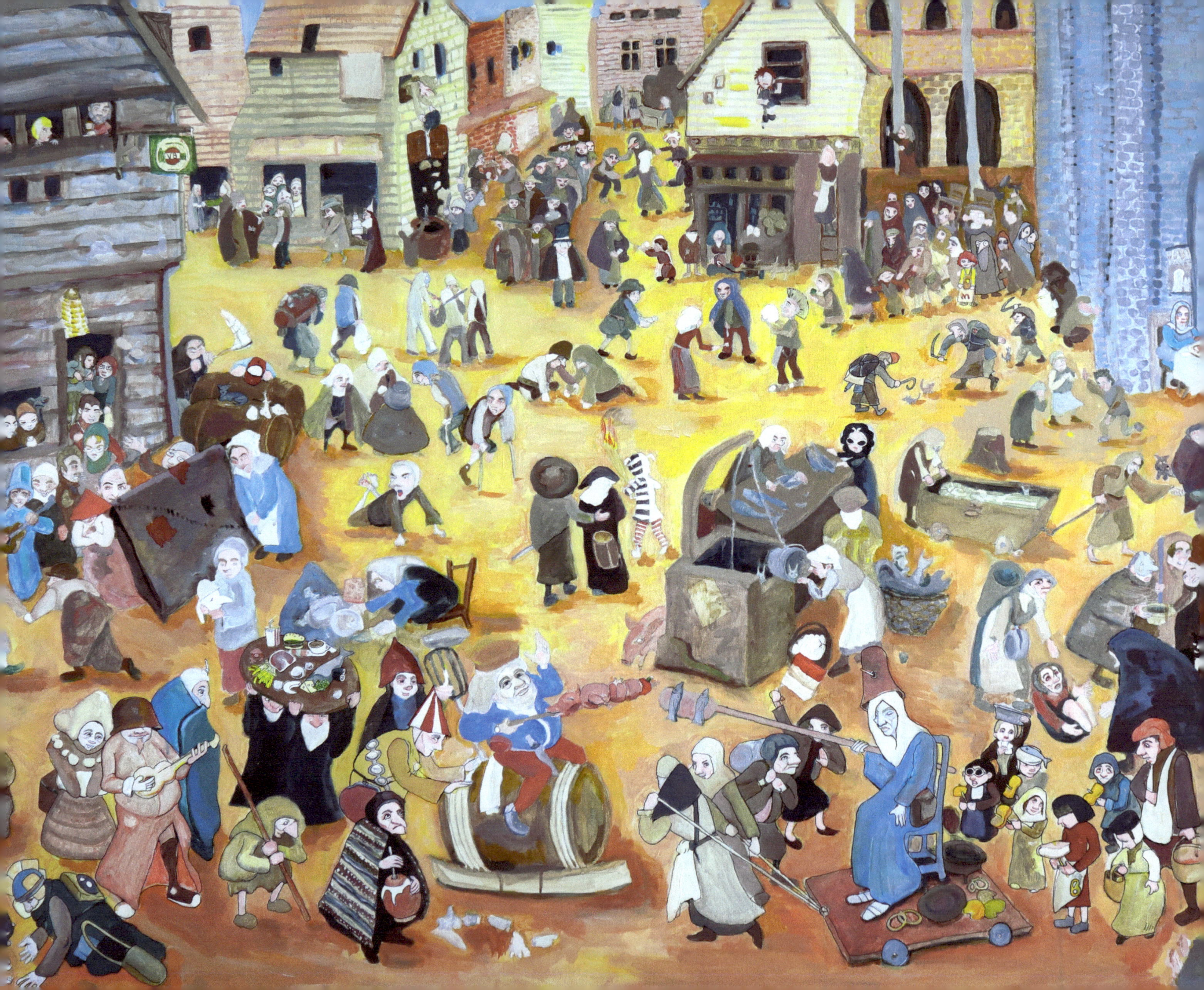

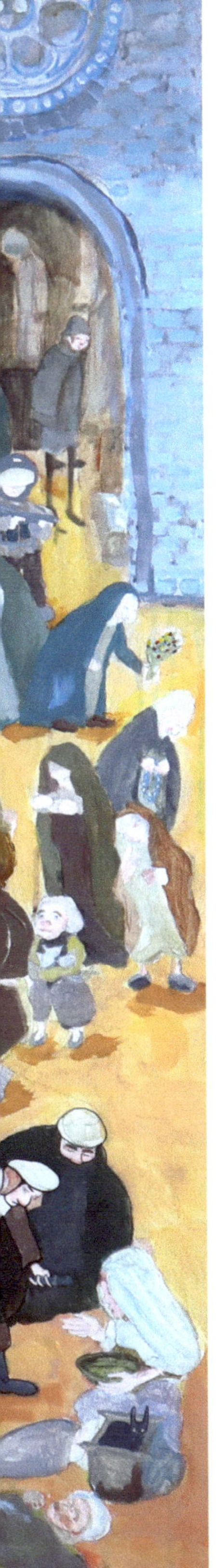

In my childhood home there was a print of *hunters in the snow*. That's where it all started.

Pieter Bruegel I (ca. 1525–1569), commonly known as Pieter Bruegel the Elder, was a painter, draftsman and printmaker who lived in Antwerp most of his life. At that time Antwerp was a flourishing centre of publishing in the Netherlands and Bruegel had a long-term association with a publishing house that produced prints on a range of subjects from parables to landscapes. Bruegel was influenced by the iconography of his predecessors such as Hieronymus Bosch and Alart Du Hameel (Ritter, 2017).

The continuing themes in Bruegel's paintings are the absurdity, wickedness and foolishness of people. Bruegels observations reflect human folly just as cartoonists, like myself, do today.

Bruegel's innovation was to transform the moralising subjects of proverbs and parables into dense images, suffused with droll humour, diabolic carnage and reflections on day-to-day life. In his painting Netherlandish Proverbs, some of the proverbs are still in use today, for example: "Swimming against the tide", "Banging one's head against a wall" and "Armed to the teeth".

I have adapted to Bruegel's style, iconography and composition. Dosing it with ample anachronisms, pop-culture, political and personal references. Just as Bruegel did in his time, I aim to highlight the absurdity, wickedness and stupidity of present day human behaviours and beliefs, particularly those that damage the planet and humanity.

The works - apart from the painting on this page - are drawn and inked on paper then scanned and digitally coloured. This book presents the illustrations with corresponding proverbs to find as well as the orignal 16th century prints for comparison. These Bruegel inspired images were created in the years between 2015-2020.

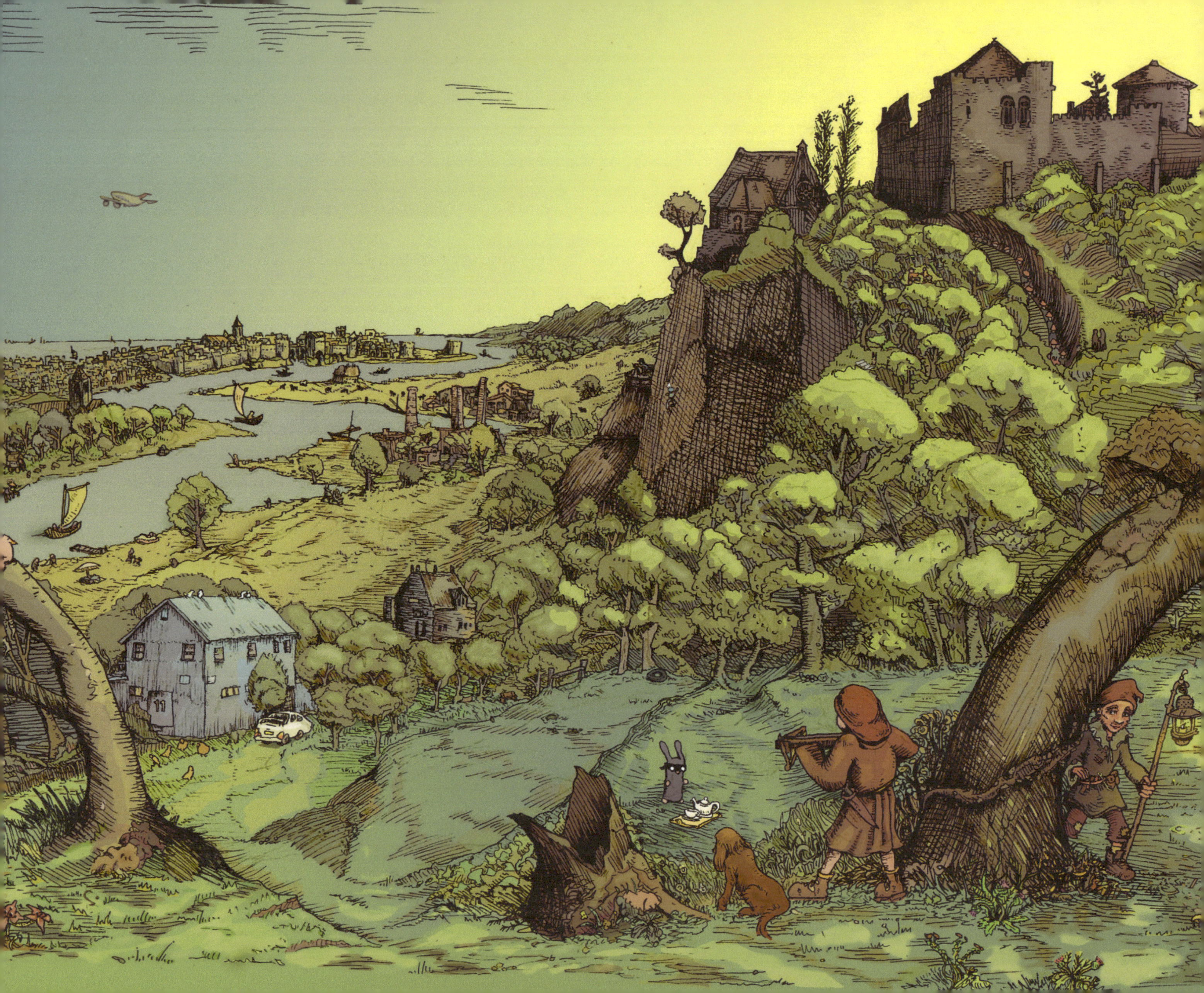
11

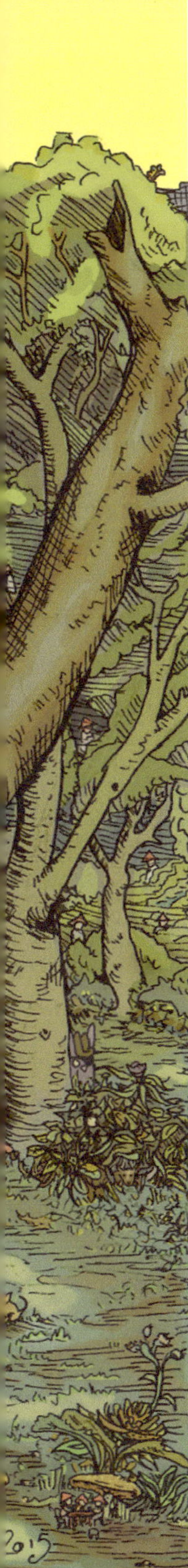

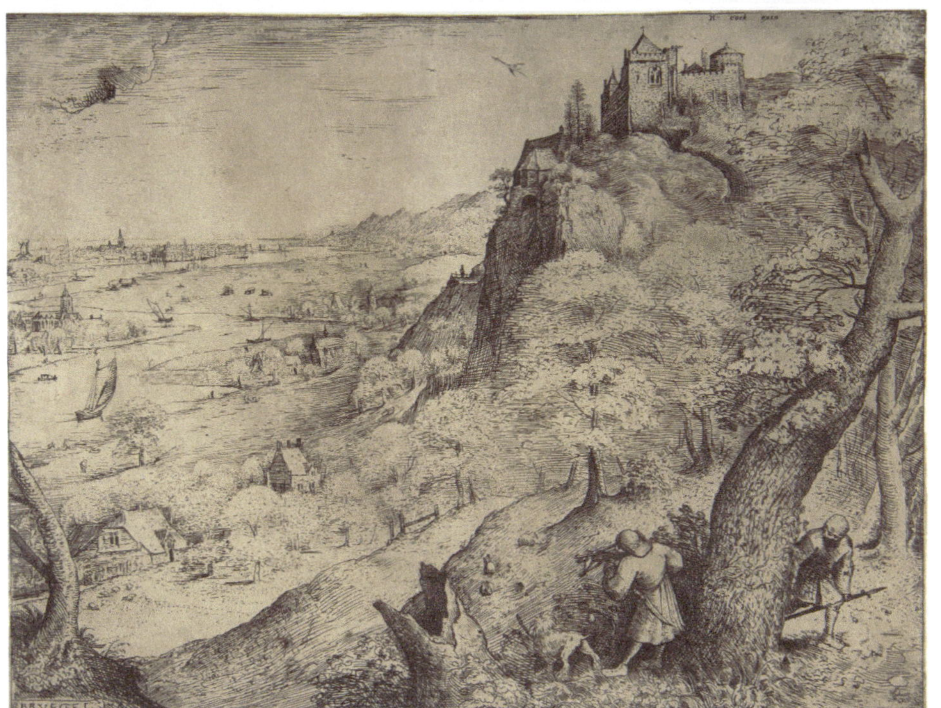

Pieter Bruegel the Elder, The rabbit hunt , 1560

Who pursues two rabbits at once will lose both

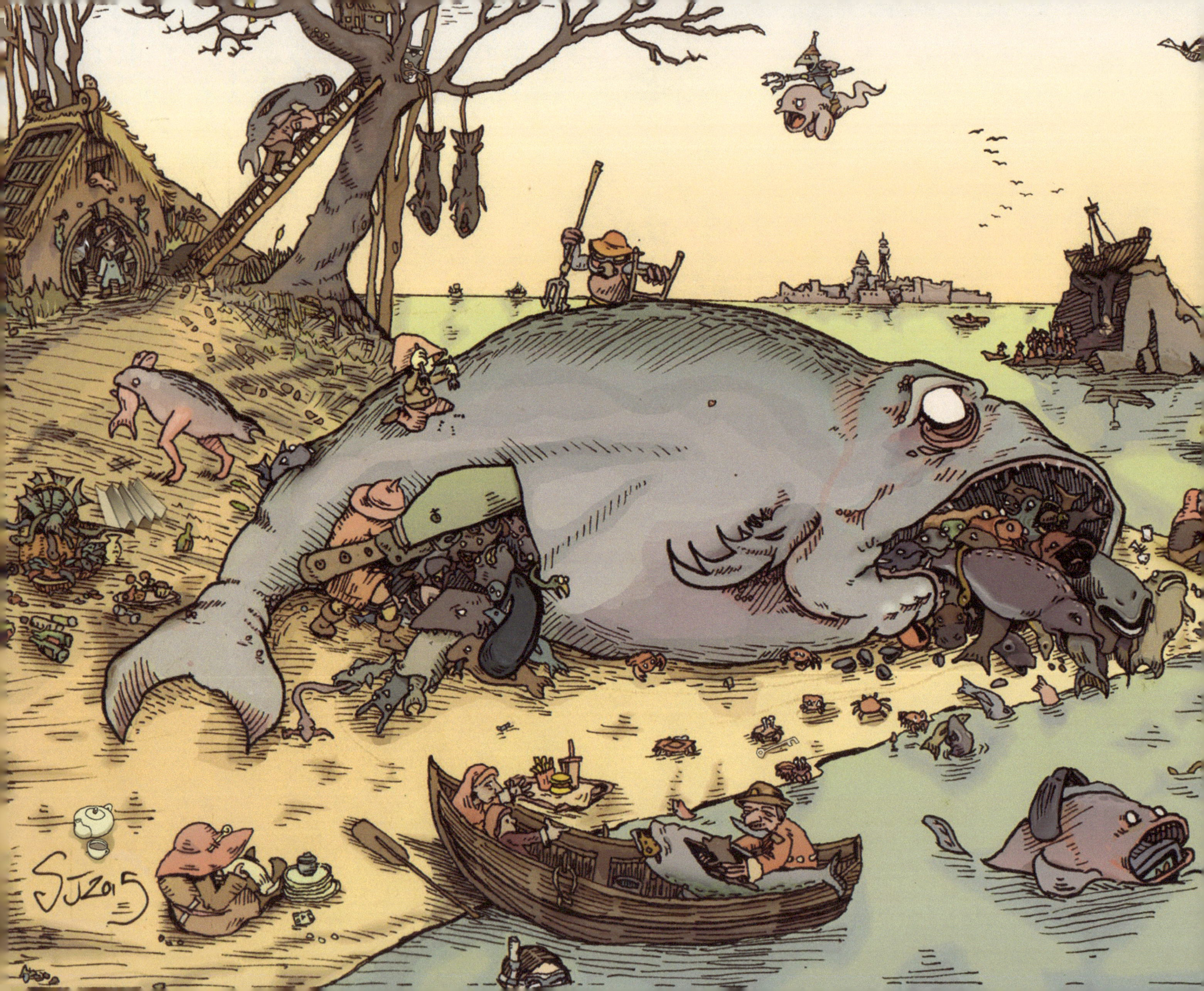
SJ2015

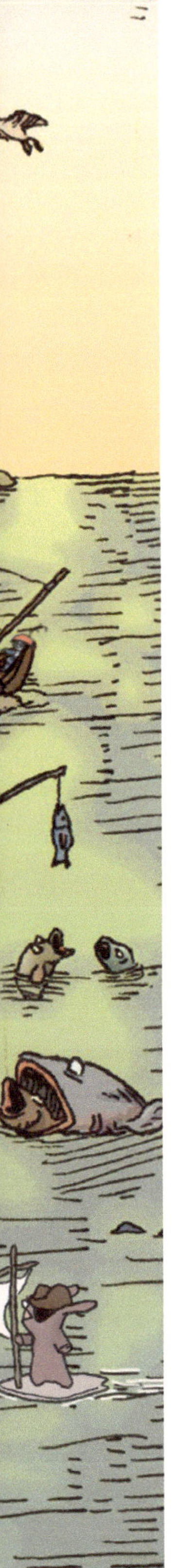

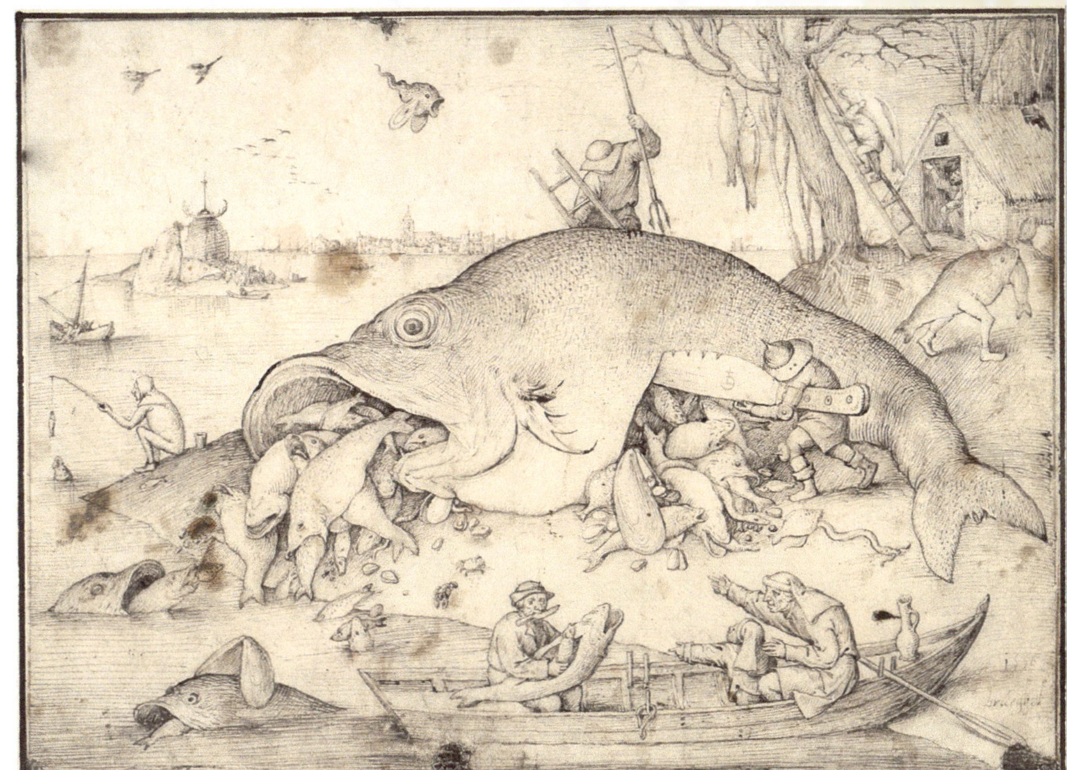

Pieter Bruegel the Elder, The big fish eat the little fish, 1556

Big fish eat the little ones.
Not my problem give me some.

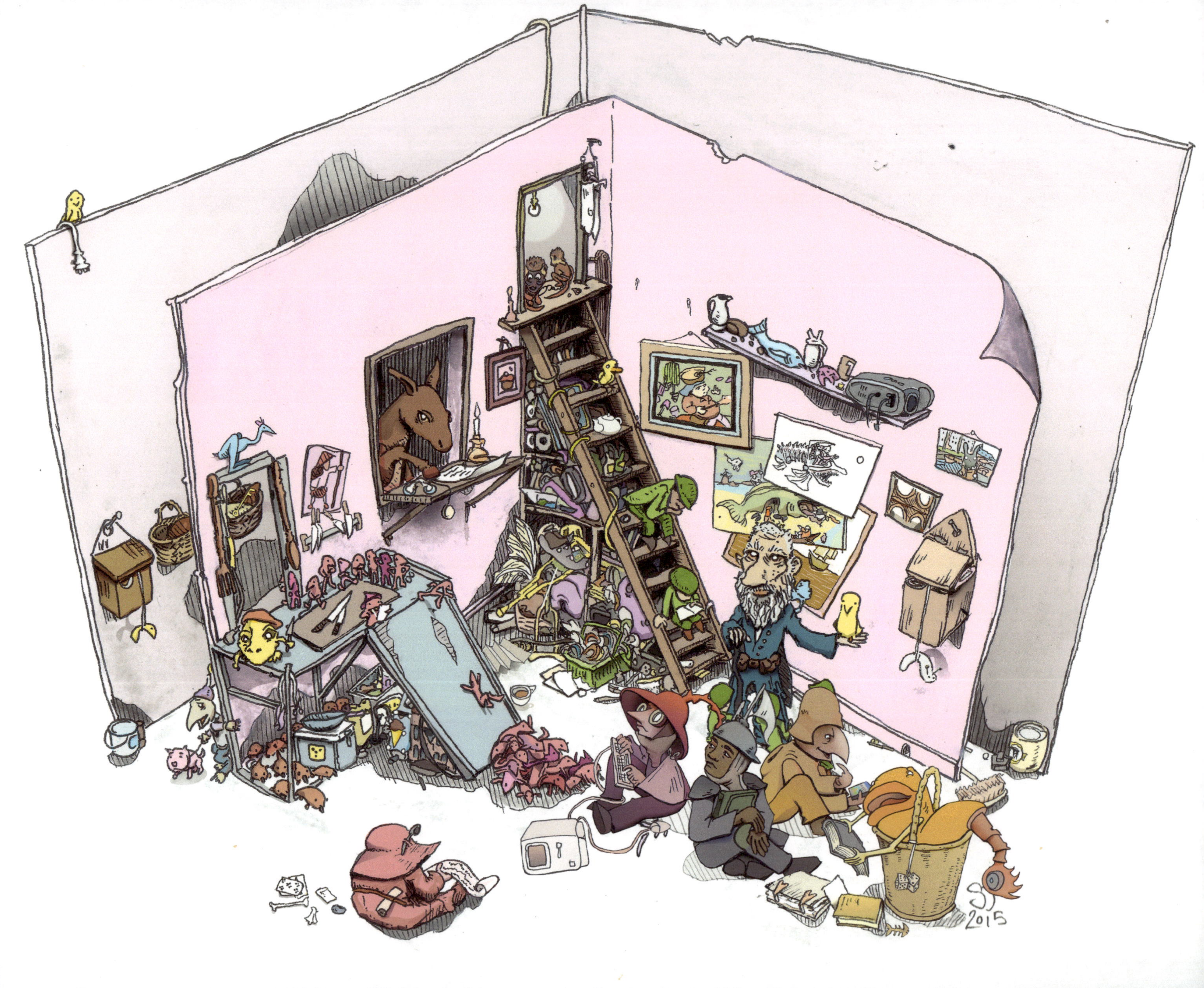
SJ
2015

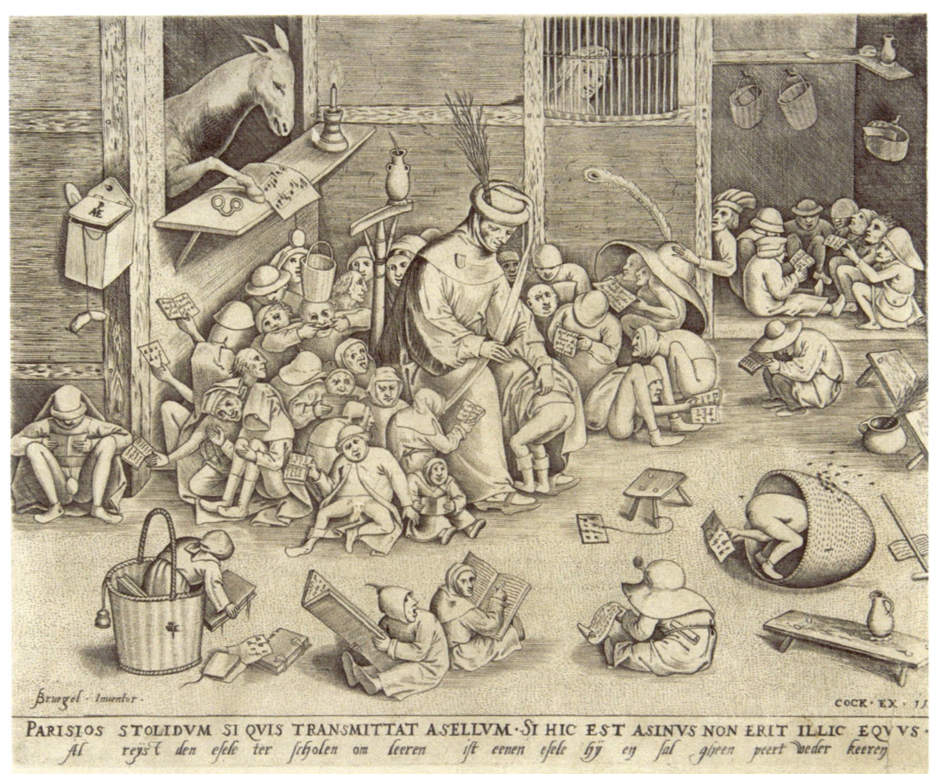

Pieter Bruegel the Elder, Ass in the school , 1556

Send a donkey to Paris, it will not come back a horse

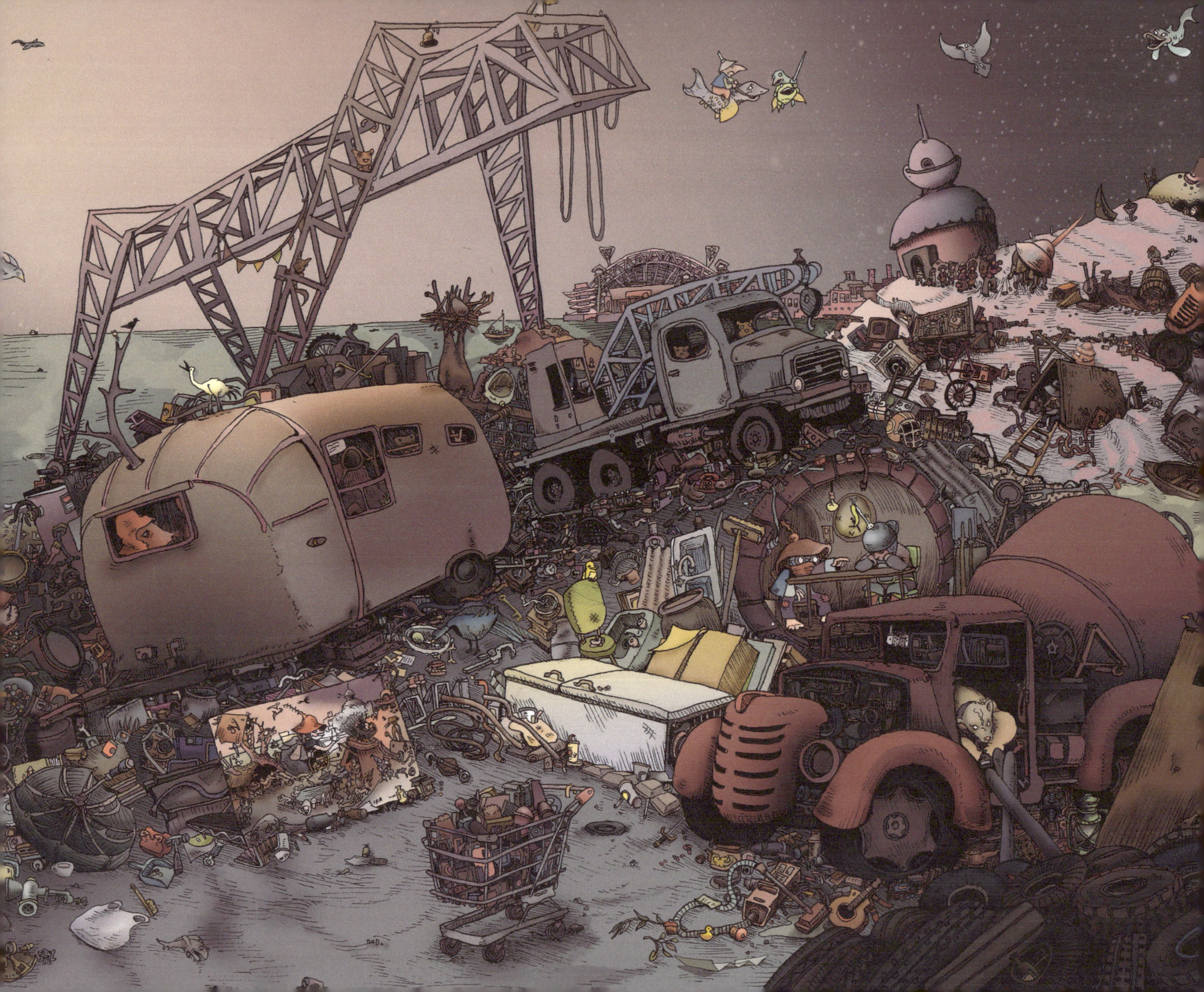

One's treasure is another's trash

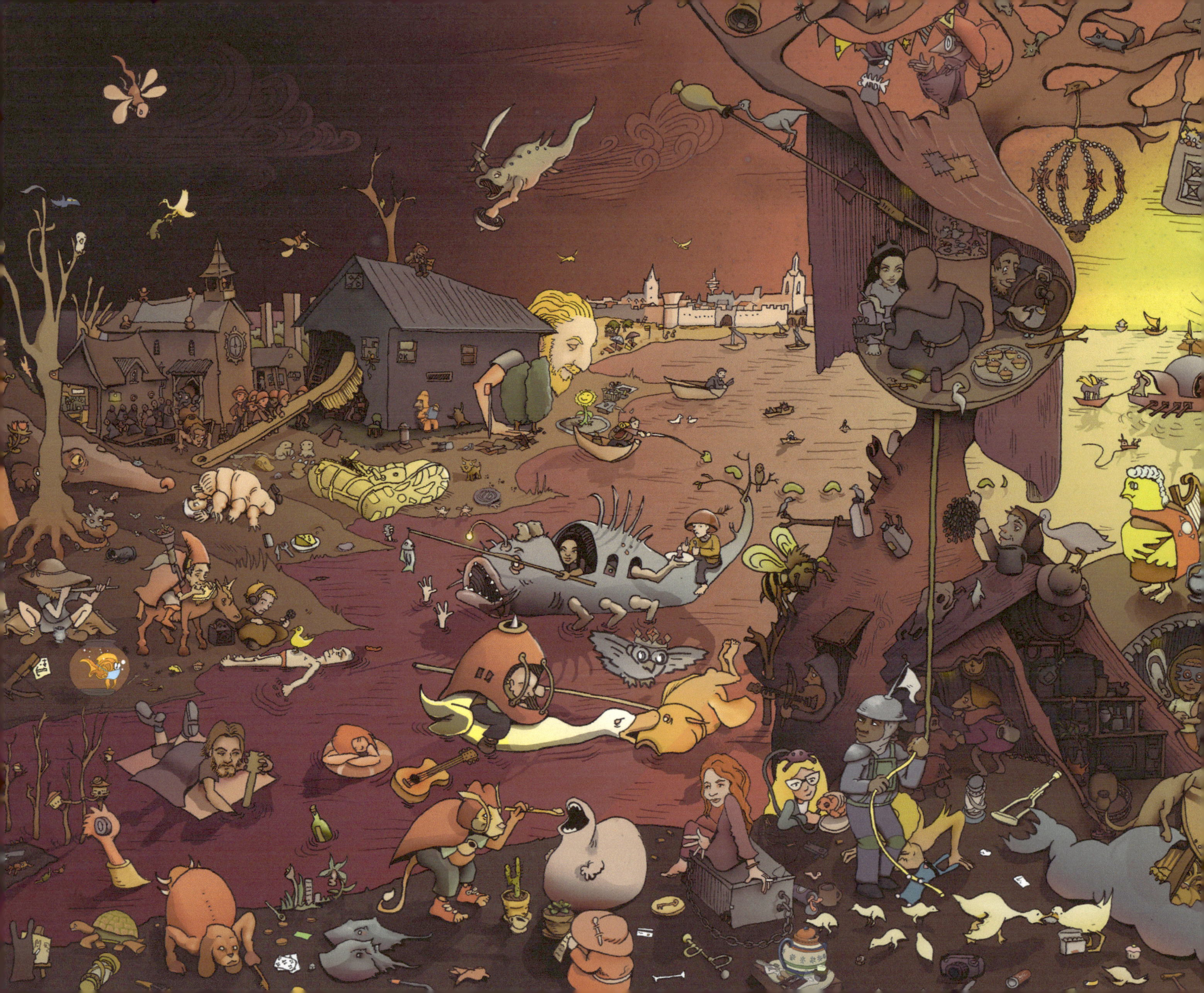

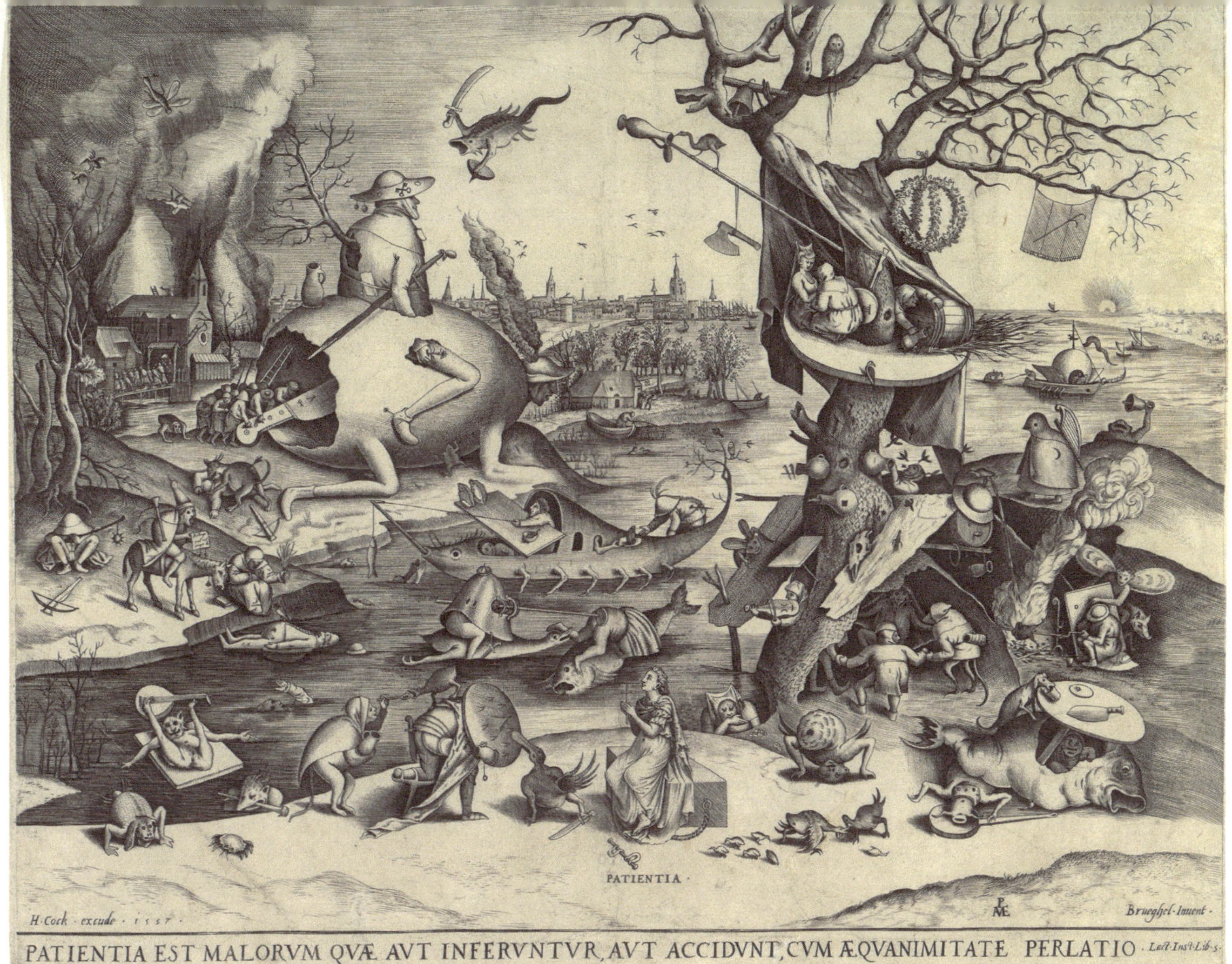

Pieter Bruegel the Elder, Patience (Patientia) 1557

Patience is a virtue.

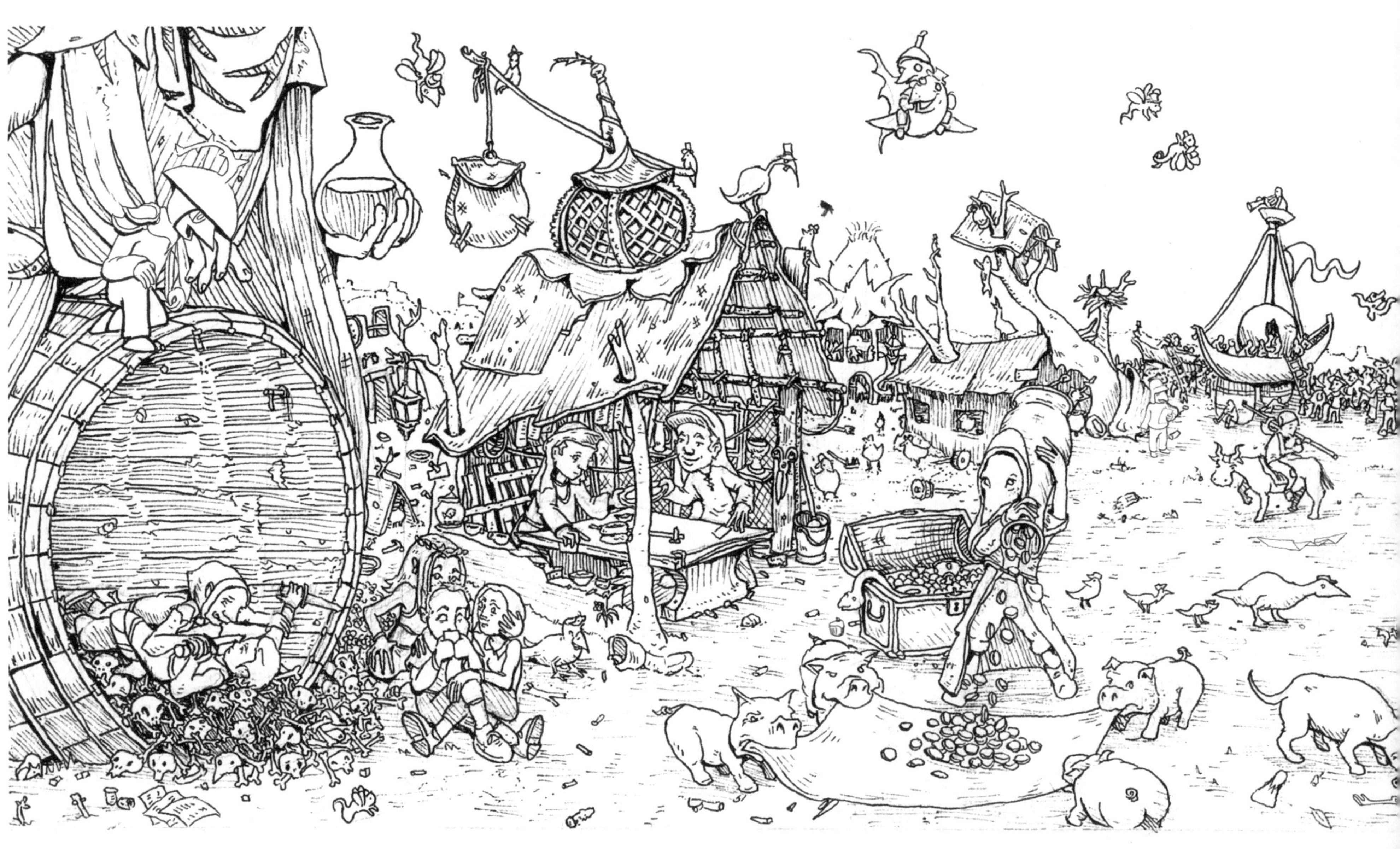

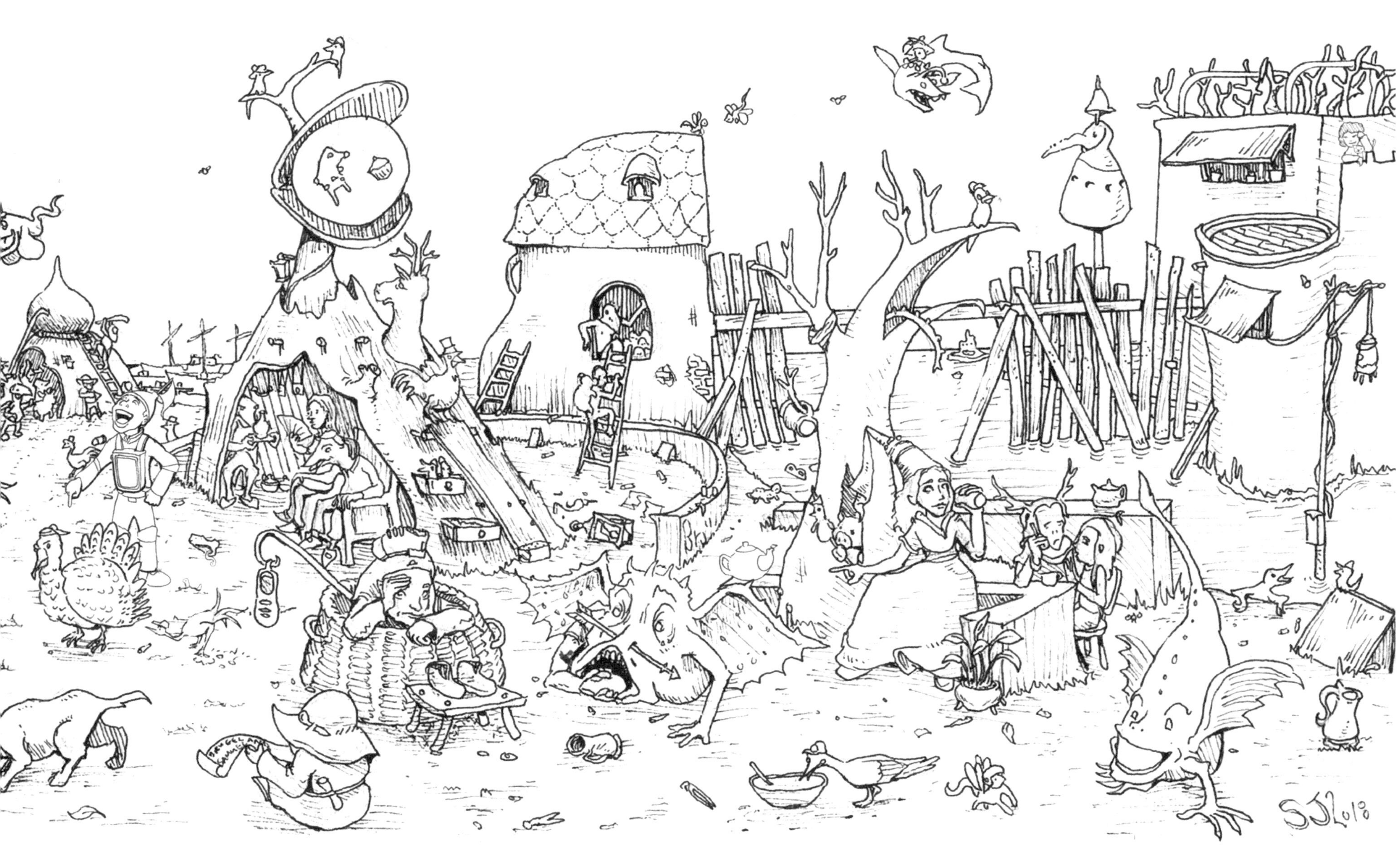
SJ2018

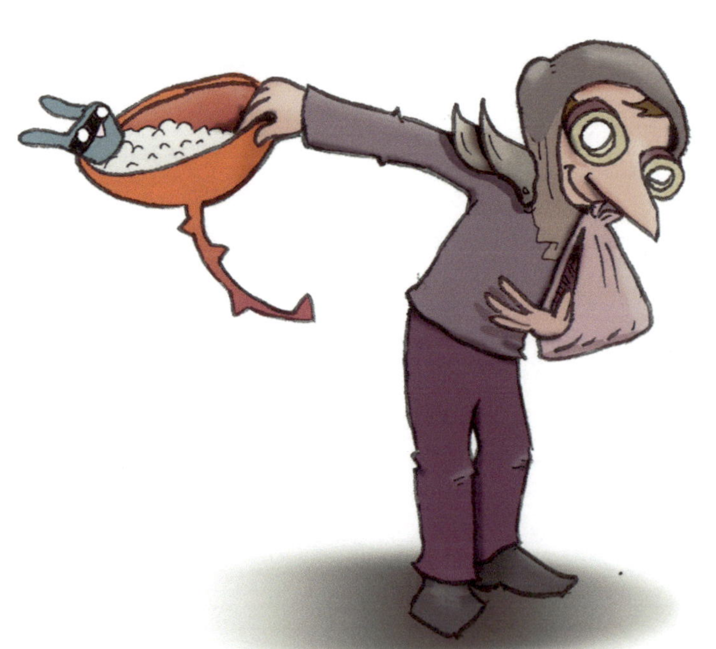

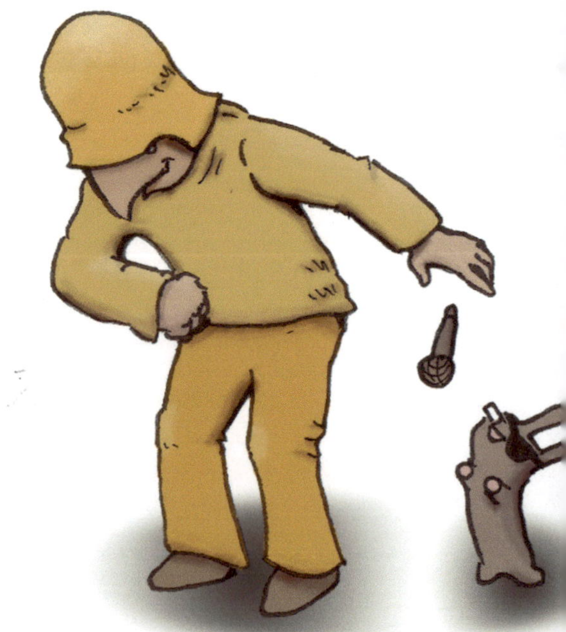

Thanks to
Marie Kohl
Thomas McNair
Lynette Russell
Dirk Brugman
Peter McNair
Maggie McNair
Joe Wilson
Chanelle Collier
Laura Hindes
Lindsay Miller
Emma Hayman
Ben Baptiste
Tawfic Elgazzar
Kohei Saiuchi
Jesse Ricketson
Pieter Van Der Heyden
and
Pieter Bruegel the Elder

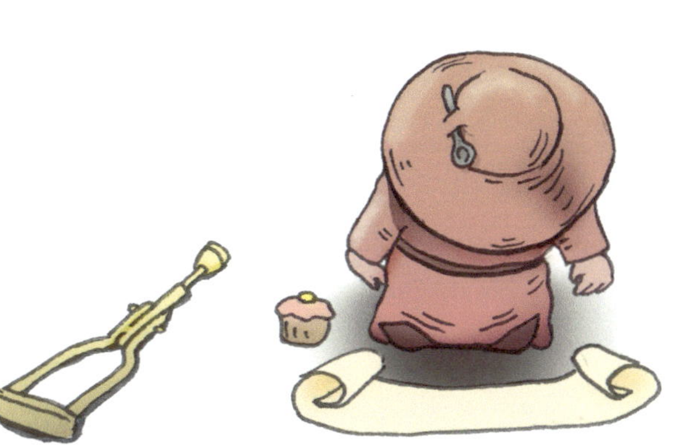

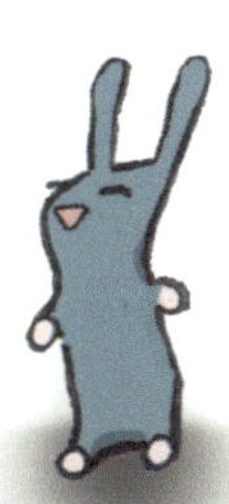

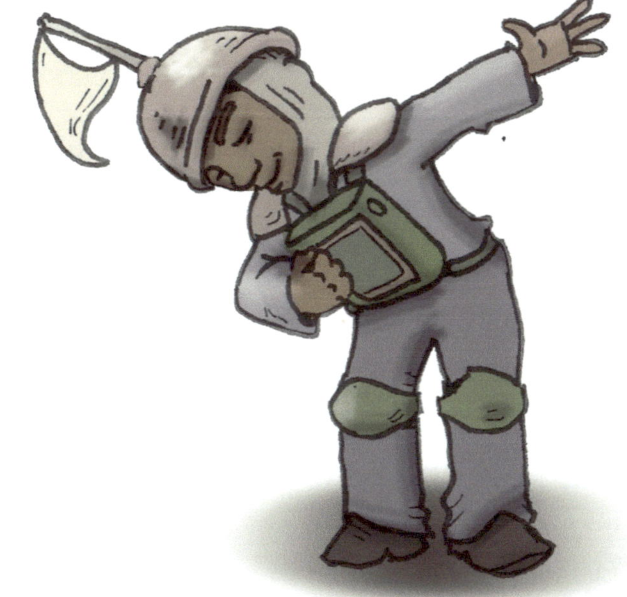

Bibliography

Charles, V. & Michel, E. (2012). Pieter Bruegel. Parkstone International, New York

Hagen, R-M. & Hagen, R. (2005). Bruegel: the complete.paintings. Taschen, Koln

Michel, E. (Ed). (2017) Pieter Bruegel: drawing the world. Hirmir, Munich

Vohringer, C. (2013). Pieter Bruegel: Masters of Netherlandish art. GmbH, Potsdam

Wright, C. (1978). The Dutch painters : 100 seventeenth century masters. Orbis Publishing, London

Samuel McNair 2021

https://samthecaricaturist.wixsite.com/samthecaricaturist

#thatsneakyrabbit

ISBN:978-0-646-83373-6

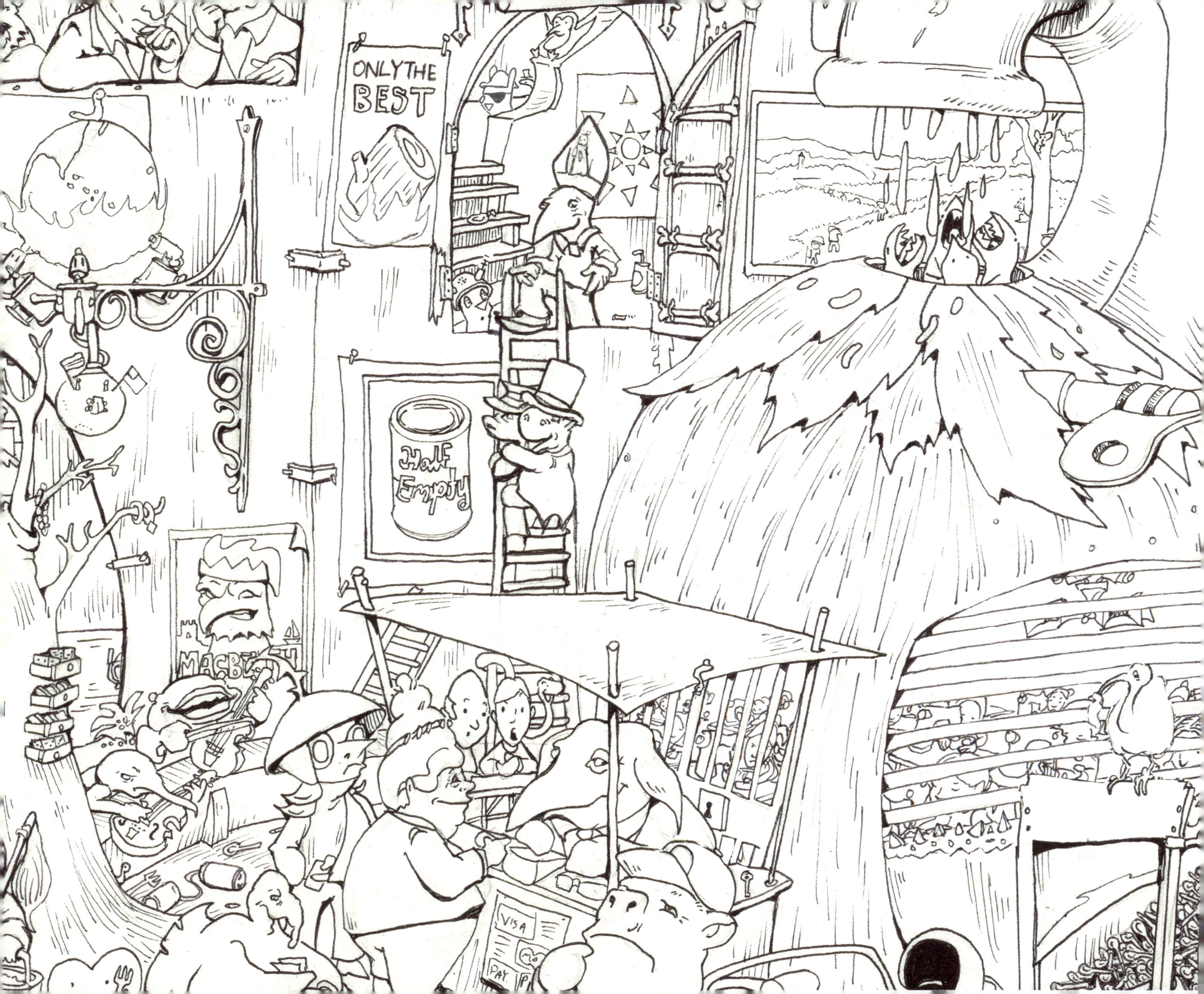
ONLY THE
BEST
Half
Empty
VISA
PAY.

Pieter Bruegel the Elder, The triumph of death, 1562

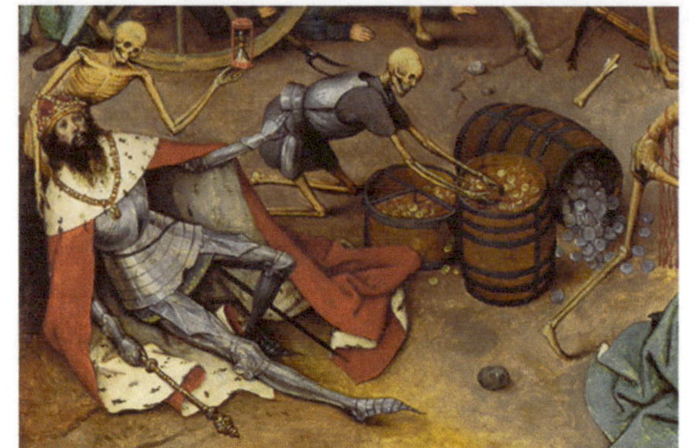

Detail

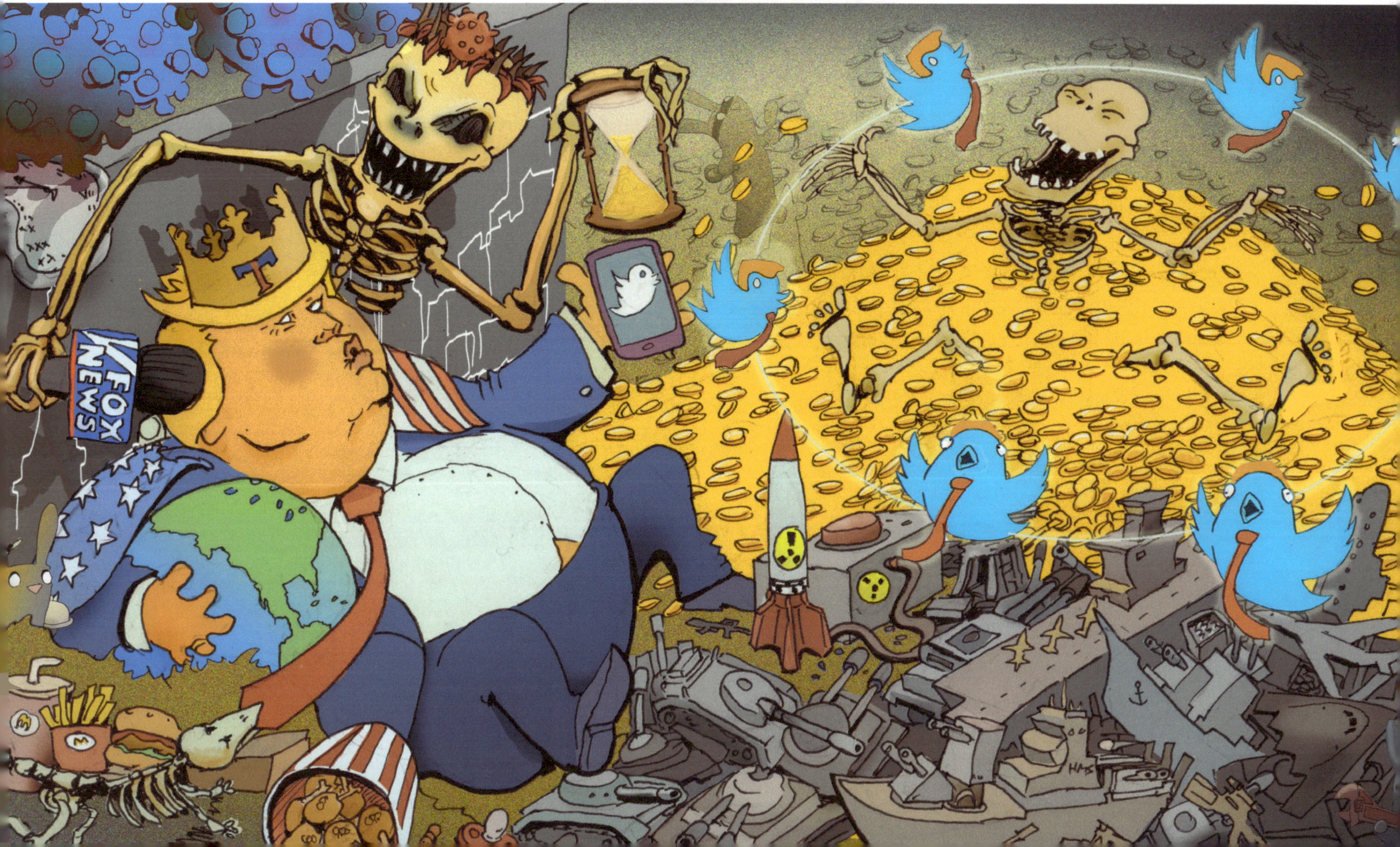

www.ingramcontent.com/pod-product-compliance
Lightning Source LLC
Chambersburg PA
CBHW040714070726
47599CB00028B/882

* 9 7 8 0 6 4 6 8 3 3 7 3 6 *